The
WHAT, WHY, AND HOW

OF HIGH-QUALITY EARLY
CHILDHOOD EDUCATION:

A GUIDE FOR ON-SITE SUPERVISION

Revised Edition

**Derry G. Koralek, Laura J. Colker,
and Diane Trister Dodge**

NATIONAL ASSOCIATION FOR THE EDUCATION OF YOUNG CHILDREN
WASHINGTON, DC

Cover design: Jack Zibulsky. *Cover photo:* Barbara Tyroler

Copyright © 1993, 1995 by Derry G. Koralek, Laura J. Colker, and Diane Trister Dodge. All rights reserved. First edition 1993. Second edition 1995. Second printing 1998. Third printing 2002. Fourth printing 2004. Fifth printing 2006.

National Association for the Education of Young Children
1509 16th Street, NW
Washington, DC 20036-1426
202–232– 8777 or 800-424-2460
www.naeyc.org

Through its publications program the National Association for the Education of Young Children (NAEYC) provides a forum for discussion of major issues and ideas in the early childhood field, with the hope of provoking thought and promoting professional growth. The views expressed or implied are not necessarily those of the Association. NAEYC thanks the authors, who donated much time and effort to develop this book as a contribution to the profession.

Library of Congress Catalog Card Number: 95-068735
ISBN 0-935989-67-6
NAEYC #336

Editor: Polly Greenberg; second edition, Carol Copple; *Book design and production:* Jack Zibulsky, Danielle Hudson, and Penny Atkins; *Copyediting:* Betty Nylund Barr; *Editorial assistance:* Julie L. Andrews and Millie Riley

Printed in the United States of America

ABOUT THE AUTHORS

Derry G. Koralek is an educational consultant who has worked with early childhood programs in a variety of settings for more than 12 years. With Diane Trister Dodge, Amy Laura Dombro, and Peter J. Pizzolongo, she wrote *Caring for Infants and Toddlers* and *Caring for Preschool Children,* two widely used CDA-based, self-instructional training programs for center-based staff. She has also coauthored a similar program for family child care providers, *Caring for Children in Family Child Care,* and one for school-age staff, *Caring for Children in School-Age Programs.* A former Head Start State Training Officer and coauthor (with Diane Trister Dodge and Cynthia Prather) of the *Guide for Education Coordinators in Head Start,* Derry has continued her association with Head Start by designing a staff-development program on working with children who are experiencing high levels of stress and by contributing to a report on the status of Head Start programs serving infants and toddlers and their families.

Laura J. Colker has written numerous publications for caregivers, family child care providers, trainers, and parents. She is, with Diane Trister Dodge, the coauthor of both *The Creative Curriculum® for Early Childhood* and *The Creative Curriculum® for Family Child Care.* Laura is a specialist in early childhood education, having directed more than 30 large-scale government contracts charged with developing curriculum, training programs, and videos. Laura was the director of content development for FOOTSTEPS, a long-running PBS series of 30 television programs on parenting. Laura is a coauthor of *Caring for Children in Family Child Care* and *Caring for Children in School-Age Programs.* Currently she is providing training for staff and supervisors at sites around the world for the new Sure Start initiative, which is a comprehensive approach to child care, based on the Head Start model, being offered to military families overseas. Laura is also a consulting editor for *Young Children.*

Diane Trister Dodge is the founder and president of Teaching Strategies, Inc., a company that seeks to improve the quality of early childhood programs. Teaching Strategies, Inc., designs practical, easy-to-use curriculum and training materials and provides staff-development services. Diane is the author of *The Creative Curriculum® for Early Childhood* and *Room Arrangement as a Teaching Strategy,* and she is the coauthor of *The Creative Curriculum® for Family Child Care,* CDA training materials, and *Constructing Curriculum for the Primary Grades.* Her professional experience includes teaching preschool and kindergarten; serving as the education coordinator for Head Start and day care programs in Mississippi and Washington, D.C.; and directing national projects in education and human services. Diane served on the Governing Board of NAEYC (1990–94) and is now a member of the Board of Directors of the National Center for the Early Childhood Work Force.

CONTENTS

FOREWORD

The U.S. Army operates the largest employer-sponsored child care program in the country at more than 134 installations. Through its Child and Youth Programs, the Army operates child development centers, family child care systems, resource-and-referral services, and school-age programs. Although each installation's approach to serving children and families is unique, they all adhere to the same high standards for quality. Since 1988 the Army has provided in-house trainers at each installation who coordinate and provide on-the-job training for all staff and family child care providers. These training and curriculum specialists spend 60 to 75% of their time in classrooms and family child care homes—observing interactions, modeling appropriate practices, making practical suggestions, providing one-on-one training, and mentoring

To provide an overview of their job tasks and expectations, in June 1989 the Army contracted with Creative Associates, International, to develop an operational handbook for these trainers. In the ensuing years, we have found this handbook to be a comprehensive, practical guide that has served the Army well. Of particular merit has been the material related to providing ongoing training in support of developmental programming. Our trainers use this guidance as the backbone of their approach to providing technical assistance.

Because this material has been so helpful to Army trainers, I am delighted that NAEYC is making this book available to the public. The authors of the original handbook have successfully adapted and expanded the material to fit the needs of any and every supervisor or trainer in an early childhood or school-age program. I am confident that *The What, Why, and How of High-Quality Early Childhood Education: A Guide for On-Site Supervision* will become a valuable tool for all who work with children.

— M.-A. Lucas
Chief, Army Child and Youth Services

ACKNOWLEDGMENTS

This publication is an adaptation of several chapters of
A Handbook for Army Education Program Specialists, prepared by
the authors for Creative Associates, International, under contract
to the U.S. Army. The chapter on programs for school-age children is based on a training program for school-age program staff
recently completed by the authors for the U.S. Army Child and
Youth Services Division. We would like to thank the Army Head-
quarters staff for their meaningful contributions as they reviewed
and provided feedback on our work. In addition, we appreciate
the guidance provided by training and curriculum specialists and
other Army child development and youth services staff in the
United States and overseas. We are especially grateful to M.-A.
Lucas, Chief, Army Child and Youth Services, for her invaluable
feedback and useful suggestions for improving the original volumes and for her willingness to have this publication made
available to supervisors and trainers who ensure the delivery of
quality services in early childhood and school-age programs.

INTRODUCTION

Learning how to provide high-quality early childhood and school-age programs is something that doesn't happen overnight. Just as it takes a toddler many tries, many frustrations, many experiments, and many successes before she can fit puzzle pieces together correctly in a frame, so too does it take time and practice to become competent in the skills needed to provide high-quality programs for children and families.

For trainers and supervisors this means working together with staff and providers to help them reach this goal. Orientation training is, of course, a prerequisite in this process. Early childhood and school-age professionals need to understand the fundamentals and components of a developmentally appropriate program so that they have a firm foundation for implementing their program. Having this knowledge base enables them to plan a program that is rooted in educational theory; for example, knowing what Piaget, Vygotsky, and Erikson, among others, have told us about the ways children grow cognitively and socioemotionally provides the information base needed to confidently operate an appropriate program for children.

We all know that in the real world, knowledge must be tempered by experience. The words *developmentally appropriate practice* by themselves carry little meaning if one does not know how to observe children to assess their current level of developmental skills. Likewise, knowing that open-ended questions encourage language development and thinking skills is nothing more than an educational tenet if one isn't skilled in asking questions such as "What could we do to the block tower to keep it from toppling over?" or "How can we set up a system for taking turns using the computer?" during the regular course of the day. Knowledge gained from formal education and orientation training must be applied in ways that reflect their true intent if they are going to positively affect the quality of care offered.

To ensure that knowledge is, in fact, translated appropriately into practice is where trainers and supervisors enter the picture once again. Training should not be viewed as a "one shot" inoculation—to be offered at orientation and then forgotten. To be effective, support should be ongoing—building on what has come before, addressing what is currently needed, and anticipating future concerns. Effective trainers and supervisors work hand-in-hand with staff and providers over time to make certain that plans, practices, and approaches are being implemented in ways that serve children and families well.

This guide is designed as a practical tool for trainers and supervisors in early childhood and school-age programs. Whether you are an education coordinator for Head Start, a training and curriculum specialist working with military child development programs, a county or state training agent, a professional trainer, the director of a private child care center, a family child care training specialist, or simply someone who is interested in promoting quality in programs for children, this guide should be of assistance to you in your work.

We encourage all readers to consult Chapter 1, which deals with several features of high-quality programs that are consistent across age groups and settings:

- *standards of quality,* as agreed upon by the profession;
- an appropriate *curriculum* framework; and
- parent involvement.

The guide addresses five specific groups of professionals:

- caregivers of infants in center-based settings;
- caregivers of toddlers in center-based settings;
- teachers of preschoolers in center-based settings;
- staff working with school-age children in center-based settings; and
- providers who care for infants, toddlers, preschoolers, and school-age children in family child care homes.

For each of the age groups and for family child care, we offer guidance on five critical program components:

- *Environment:* the arrangement of furniture, equipment, and materials—indoors and outdoors—in ways that promote positive behavior and learning
- *Equipment and materials:* the selection and display of materials that address children's developmental skills and needs and that reflect children's interests
- *Program structure:* a schedule and daily routines designed to respond to children's developmental needs and that allow them to pursue their interests
- *Activities and experiences:* the daily program of activities and opportunities offered that promote children's learning and growth
- *Supportive interactions:* the supportive manner in which adults respond to children, guide their behavior, encourage their explorations, and promote social development

Within each of these five components, we offer guidance on what you, as a trainer or supervisor, should see when you walk into an effective center-based program or family child care home. In addition, we discuss why these items, interactions, or ap-

proaches are indicators of quality. Following this, we present a number of warning signs to watch for that might indicate a potential problem. For each warning sign, we suggest possible underlying causes for the problem, as well as concrete suggestions for what you, as a trainer or supervisor, might implement as corrective actions. Each chapter concludes with a list of relevant print and audiovisual resources that should further assist you in your work.

When using this guide, feel free to skip around and consult those chapters that cover your work area. If you offer staff development for child care centers serving infants and toddlers, for example, Chapters 2 and 3 will be of most value to you. Similarly, if you work with family child care providers, Chapter 6 will hold the most interest for you. Trainers or supervisors who work with both center staff and family child care providers will probably find all six chapters to be relevant to their needs. You are, of course, encouraged to read and make use of the entire guide—no matter who your target audience is—because each chapter presents a different slant to the same topics.

Consider this guide a working tool. The items covered here are by no means exhaustive; rather, they are meant to focus your thinking and to spark your creative ideas and approaches to supporting professional development. All of us in the field share the desire to provide programs for children and families that reflect the highest standards of quality. This guide is intended to help you help staff and providers come a step closer to realizing that goal.

CHAPTER ONE

Establishing the Foundation

Standards of quality _____

The quality of an early childhood or school-age program can be determined by the degree to which it meets the standards of the profession. Whether carried out in center-based or family–home settings serving infants, toddlers, preschoolers and school-age children, the program should be based on theories and principles of child development and accepted best practices of early childhood and school-age programs. Seven key indicators of quality are described below.

The program is based on an understanding of child development

When a program is based on child development theory, it is considered "developmentally appropriate." As defined by the National Association for the Education of Young Children, a developmentally appropriate program is one that is planned and carried out based on a knowledge of how children grow and what they can do—socially, emotionally, cognitively, and physically—at each stage of development. Children are learning new skills and developing special interests as they take on typical growth tasks at each stage of life. In addition to having their own individual timetables of growth and development, children bring their own special interests, life experiences, strengths, and needs. A quality program is therefore based on not only what is appropriate for a given age group but also what is individually appropriate for each child.*

A program that is *age appropriate* takes into consideration the normal sequences of growth typical of children within a given age group. Infants and toddlers, for example, learn by experiencing the environment using all of their senses—seeing, tasting, hearing, smelling, and feeling—and by moving around their environment as they develop the ability to crawl and walk. The key to an appropriate curriculum for infants and toddlers is the relationships they build with the adults who care for them. This is the

*Bredekamp, S. (Ed.). (1987). *Developmentally appropriate practice in early childhood programs serving children from birth through age 8* (exp. ed.). Washington, DC: NAEYC.

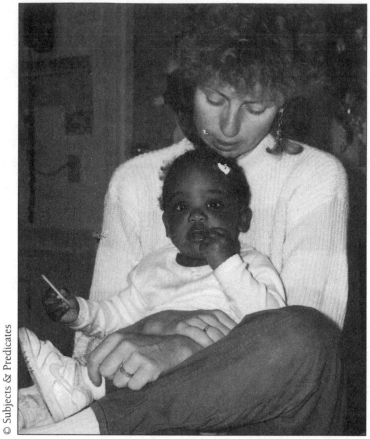

A program that is individually appropriate recognizes that each child is a unique person with individual patterns of growth, individual preferences for activities, and different family backgrounds.

best way for children under three to learn about themselves and the world. Adults who work with preschool children understand that they are active, social individuals who have lots of ideas they want to share. Preschoolers are developing friendships, and they benefit most when offered a variety of activity choices, such as dramatic play, block building, art, toys, puzzles, exploring sand and water, cooking, music and movement, and a rich and ever-changing selection of good books.

School-age children are primarily involved with expanding their worlds beyond the family unit and gradually growing toward independence. They have clear ideas about what they like to do during their out-of-school hours, are eager to spend time with peers, and are able to make plans and carry them out with minimal adult supervision. Staff working with this age group need to involve the children in planning a variety of interest areas, games, sports, and activities that allow children to use their physical, cognitive, and socioemotional skills.

A program that is *individually appropriate* recognizes that each child is a unique person with individual patterns of growth, individual preferences for activities, and different family backgrounds. No two children develop on the same schedule or in exactly the same sequence. One child may walk earlier but begin using words later than other children of the same age. Some children will spend hours playing with blocks and wheel toys; others prefer quieter activities, such as puzzles and books. In quality programs staff members recognize that children are individuals, and they do not expect each child to conform to a rigid timetable of growth or engage in the same activities.

The program is individualized to meet the needs of every child

Individualizing the program promotes the growth and development of each child. Knowing what to expect at each stage of development enables staff and providers to plan a program of activities that is appropriate for the children in their care, yet individualizing requires more than a good understanding of normal child development. Although most children go through a consistent sequence in their development of skills and understandings, the rate at which children progress through these stages may differ considerably. Additionally, each child has unique experiences, interests, and cultural values that must be recognized and respected.

In a quality program, staff and providers use a variety of strategies to help them learn as much as they can about each child's development, interests, and family background. They talk with parents, observe children's daily interactions in the program, and document what children learn, using checklists, anecdotal records, and portfolios of children's work. They use this information to make changes to the environment, to plan activities, and to design strategies to promote each child's optimal growth and development. One of the easiest ways to individualize a program is to plan a variety of developmentally appropriate activities every day and allow children to make choices. The materials, interactions, and activities in a quality program should reflect what makes each child a unique individual.

The physical environment is safe and orderly, and it contains varied and stimulating toys and materials

A quality program ensures that children are safe while they are away from their parents. This means that the adults continually check the indoor and outdoor play areas to be sure that no hazards exist and that children can freely explore and move around without endangering themselves or others. It also means that children are supervised at all times to prevent accidents and that adults respond immediately to any emergencies.

Children's health is a primary concern in quality programs. Standard procedures exist for diapering, toileting, hand washing, and food service. Adults follow good nutrition practices in planning and serving snacks and meals and eat with children family style to make mealtime a social and enjoyable period of the day. Children are involved in food preparation in age-appropriate ways.

In quality programs the environment is carefully arranged and stocked with toys and materials appropriate for the children in the group. Adults regularly rotate these learning materials and toys and add new ones as children's interests and abilities change.

Children may select activities and materials that interest them, and they learn by being actively involved

Quality programs help children develop independence and view themselves as competent learners. Toys and materials are kept on low shelves where children can reach what they need and learn to return them when they are finished. Giving children choices helps them learn to make decisions and ensures that they can participate in activities that interest them. Children learn best when they can explore concrete materials and when they can share their ideas and questions with other children and with caring adults. In a quality program you will see children who are involved and active and who are talking and playing freely with others.

Adults show respect for children's needs and ideas and talk with them in caring ways

The quality of a program is most evident in the ways that adults work with children. Adults respond quickly to children's needs and communications. Infants and toddlers need adults who will hold them, soothe them, and provide caring attention to ensure their emotional and physical comfort. As children get older they thrive around adults who will listen to their ideas, respond to their questions, and help them learn to think for themselves.

Young children are developing self-control and learning what behavior is acceptable and what is not acceptable. They need adults who guide their behavior in positive ways that build self-esteem. This means not punishing children, belittling them, or yelling at them when they make mistakes, but setting clear and consistent limits. Adults patiently explain the rules to children, redirect them to more acceptable behavior, and help them learn to solve problems on their own.

Parents feel respected and are encouraged to participate in the program

In quality programs staff and providers develop partnerships with parents because parents have both a right and a responsibility to participate in decisions about their children's care. Parents know their children best and can share valuable information about their children's development. Staff and providers have specialized training in child development and daily opportunities to see how

Quality programs are planned and implemented by people who are skilled and knowledgeable about caring for children in child care settings, and quality programs are based on child development.

children react to a group situation. In quality programs staff and providers greet parents by name, take time to talk about the program and their children's progress, invite parents to participate in activities or special events, and share resources with parents. When parents and staff share their knowledge and work together, children benefit most from their experience.

Staff members have specialized training in child development, education, and appropriate programming

Quality programs are planned and implemented by people who are skilled and knowledgeable about caring for children in child care settings. These individuals have attended workshops, courses, and staff-development programs and have read through practical resources. They have developed the skills and knowledge defined by the profession as essential to providing competent care and education.

Curriculum

Quality programs have adopted a clearly defined curriculum framework that guides the daily program of activities. Adults who work with children must have a good understanding of how children learn; be able to respond to children as they explore materials, ask questions, and solve problems; and have the ability to make decisions that meet the needs of the group and of each child in their care. On a daily basis they ask themselves questions such as the following:

- Should I intervene, or should I step back and let the child try to resolve a problem?
- What questions can I ask to help the child think through the problem and come up with a solution?
- Is the child ready for these materials, or will they prove frustrating?
- Is the physical environment working, or do I need to modify it?

A curriculum provides the framework that helps staff and providers answer these questions.*

Components of a curriculum

An early childhood curriculum is not easily defined or explained. Ask several people to give you their definition of curriculum in early childhood and you will get a variety of responses. Some show you a book of themes and activities that they follow each year. Others say that they like to be flexible and simply

*Dodge, D.T., & Colker, L.J. (1992). *The creative curriculum for early childhood* (3rd ed.). Washington, DC: Teaching Strategies, Inc.

respond to what interests the children day by day. Curriculum is actually somewhere between these two extremes. It is the framework that guides adults in creating an environment, in planning appropriate activities, and in facilitating children's growth and development. Within this framework, staff and providers can respond to children's individual interests and day-to-day experiences. An early childhood curriculum that gives guidance on planning the daily program has the following six components.

- A statement of philosophy—a description of the educational theories and child development principles underlying the curriculum's approach to early childhood education. An appropriate curriculum for child development programs is based on an understanding of how young children learn and how they develop socially, emotionally, cognitively, and physically.

- A statement of goals and objectives—clearly defined, realistic goals and objectives that cover all areas of development and that outline what children can be expected to achieve as infants, toddlers, and preschoolers. Goals and objectives are used to plan activities and experiences with a specific purpose in mind and to assess each child's progress.

- Guidance on creating the physical environment—specific guidance on how to arrange indoor and outdoor space to support children's growth and development. The curriculum should specify how best to set up areas of the classroom or family child care home, what materials and equipment are appropriate, and how they should be grouped and displayed.

- An educational approach—a clear explanation of how to plan and implement the curriculum. Having established goals and objectives and a learning environment that supports the program, staff and providers benefit from a curriculum that defines their role in observing children's interactions, facilitating their play, and extending their learning.

- Suggestions for developmentally appropriate activities—suggested activities that can be used in planning for and responding to the interests and needs of children. Activities are organized in a variety of ways, depending on the curriculum model (e.g., by themes or units, or by interest areas).

- A meaningful role for parents—recognition that parents are their children's first and primary teachers. A developmentally appropriate program curriculum, therefore, includes guidance on ensuring a meaningful role for parents in the daily program and offers suggestions for sharing the curriculum with parents.

School-age programs may view "curriculum" as the framework that guides what children do in a school setting, rather than during their out-of-school time. However, effective school-age programs are also guided by a curriculum framework. Staff create an environment, provide materials and equipment, and plan activities and experiences that support the program's philosophy and goals for children. They encourage children's growing independence and help children develop a realistic self-image.

Selecting a developmentally appropriate curriculum

NAEYC has established guidelines for developing curriculum or deciding whether a curriculum is developmentally appropriate. These guidelines can be helpful in assessing the appropriateness of your curriculum for the group of children served. The guidelines are also useful in determining whether the curriculum you are using is being implemented in a way that is responsive to the individual needs, interests, and developmental levels of the children.

Use the following questions to assess the appropriateness of your curriculum. If you can answer affirmatively each of the 20 questions, then the curriculum you are using is probably developmentally appropriate. If it does not meet these criteria, you may want to consider a new curriculum for the programs you supervise.

1. Does it promote interactive learning and encourage the child's construction of knowledge?

2. Does it help achieve social, emotional, physical, and cognitive goals and promote democratic values?

3. Does it encourage development of positive feelings and dispositions toward learning while leading to acquisition of knowledge and skills?

4. Is it meaningful for these children? Is it relevant to the children's lives? Can it be made more relevant by relating it to a personal experience children have had, or can they easily gain direct experience with it?

5. Are the expectations realistic and attainable at this time, or could the children more easily and efficiently acquire the knowledge or skills later on?

6. Is it of interest to children and to the teacher?

7. Is it sensitive to and respectful of cultural and linguistic diversity? Does it expect, allow, and appreciate individual differences? Does it promote positive relationships with families?

8. Does it build on and elaborate children's current knowledge and abilities?

9. Does it lead to conceptual understanding by helping children construct their own understanding in meaningful contexts?

10. Does it facilitate integration of content across traditional subject-matter areas?

11. Is the information presented accurate and credible according to the recognized standards of the relevant discipline?

12. Is this content worth knowing? Can it be learned by these children efficiently and effectively now?

13. Does it encourage active learning and allow children to make meaningful choices?

14. Does it foster children's exploration and inquiry, rather than focusing on "right" answers or "right" ways to complete a task?

15. Does it promote the development of higher order abilities, such as thinking, reasoning, problem solving, and decisionmaking?

16. Does it promote and encourage social interaction among children and adults?

17. Does it respect children's physiological needs for activity, sensory stimulation, fresh air, rest, hygiene, and nourishment/elimination?

18. Does it promote feelings of psychological safety, security, and belonging?

19. Does it provide experiences that promote feelings of success, competence, and enjoyment of learning?

20. Does it permit flexibility for children and adults?

Reprinted with permission from *Reaching potentials: Appropriate curriculum and assessment for young children: Volume 1* (p. 22). S. Bredekamp & T. Rosegrant, Eds. (1992). Washington, DC: NAEYC.

Parent involvement

Quality early childhood and school-age programs value and actively promote a partnership with children's families. The younger the child, the more critical it is for programs to establish a relationship of trust and respect with each child's family. For the staff of school-age programs, often lacking direct contact with children's teachers, parents are a key source of information about the child's school experiences. Ongoing communication with a child's parents provides insights into the child's unique characteristics, strengths, needs, and interests. In situations in which the staff's or provider's cultural backgrounds are very different from a child's, parents are the best resource for learning about the expectations and communication patterns that influence how the child relates to others and interprets experiences.

When parents are involved in the program in meaningful ways, everyone benefits. Parents feel that they are part of a team and are not abandoning their children during the day. The more parents learn about the program and its goals for their children, the more they can extend and reinforce learning and development at home. Staff and providers can be more effective when parents share insights about their children and contribute to the program by donating their time and resources to enrich the curriculum. And children benefit the most when the significant adults in their lives are working together to give them the support and guidance they need to grow and develop. Trust is more easily established when children see that their worlds are closely linked.

Parent involvement (cont'd)

To involve parents in the program in meaningful ways, staff and providers must appreciate the importance of parent involvement and know how to achieve it. Listed below are some examples of strategies that promote a partnership with families.

What you should see	Why
parents greeted by name when they bring children and pick them up	Parents feel accepted and valued when they have a personal relationship with the adults who care for their children during the day.
conversations about the child's day (e.g., a special interest, accomplishment, or anecdote)	Informal daily communication is one of the best ways to keep parents informed about their child's life at the program.
concern shown for a parent's feelings when separation is upsetting or the child has had a difficult day	Genuine concern for the parent's needs and feelings builds a strong bond and helps parents to cope.
a parent bulletin board or message center featuring this week's schedule, current menus, and photographs of children engaged in activities, and regularly updated with announcements of important events	A bulletin board or message center tells parents that they are important and the staff or provider wants to keep them informed.
a parent corner filled with pamphlets, articles, and other resources of interest to the parents	Including a special place for parents conveys the message that their needs are considered important and that resources are available to help them.
a system for regularly communicating with parents about the program and about each child	For infants and toddlers, daily communication about routines reassures parents that they are completely involved in their children's care. For older children, communication might occur weekly or as needed.
information shared with parents about what children are doing and learning and how parents can build on these experiences	When parents are informed about the program, they can extend and reinforce children's learning and experiences, talk with children about what they are doing, and help children expand their skills and interests. Children feel secure and supported when they know there is a connection between home and the program.
family members encouraged to participate in the program by sharing a skill or interest or some aspect of their cultural heritage	Family members often have a lot they can contribute to enrich the program experiences. Inviting them to share their knowledge and skills conveys respect.

What you should see	Why
regularly scheduled parent meetings to discuss topics of interest to parents, to hear guest speakers, and to learn about the program	The more parents understand the program's philosophy, the more they can support their children's growth and development.
parent conferences held to share information and progress on each child; documentation of the results added in each child's folder	Parent conferences are an excellent way to learn about each child in order to individualize the program.
family events, sponsored by the program, that involve children, parents, and staff in enjoyable activities	Relationships between children and parents are supported when they have opportunities to have fun together.

Signs that parents are not meaningfully involved

Assessing the level of parent involvement requires more than a visit to the program. Some of the indicators are subtle and take time to uncover. If you note any of the warning signs listed below, the staff or provider may need your support and encouragement to successfully involve families in the program.

Warning signs	Why this might be happening	How you can help
parents complaining that the program is not challenging the children or preparing them to be successful in school and in life	Staff or providers may not know how to explain the program to parents and may feel judged when parents make suggestions.	Provide resources that will help staff and providers to articulate the program's philosophy, including summaries of research studies on the long-term benefits of a developmental approach.
parents viewing staff or providers as the experts and feeling as if they have no role in the program	This may result from their own experiences and cultural perspective on clear role definitions.	Help staff or providers to plan an open house at which parents can experience the program through hands-on activities and learn about the importance of their involvement.
parents dropping off their children and leaving without staying to talk or to observe the program	Staff or providers may have conveyed the message that it is better for the children if the transition is brief.	Discuss the significance of separation for children of different ages and for adults, and offer specific ways to help parents ease the transition.

Warning signs	Why this might be happening	How you can help
no bulletin board with announcements for parents, or a bulletin board that is rarely changed or updated	Staff or providers may not see this as part of their responsibility and fail to value its importance.	Plan a workshop to create a bulletin board or to make posters that explain what children are learning from different routines, interest areas, and experiences.
poor attendance of parents at parent meetings; staff or providers stating that parents are not interested	Attending evening meetings may be impossible for families because of job responsibilities or a lack of caregivers for young children.	Suggest developing a questionnaire to seek parents' ideas on appropriate topics and times for parent meetings. Offer alternative ways to involve family members, such as potluck meals at the end of the day or on weekends. Prepare videotapes of speakers that parents can check out if they can't attend meetings.
parent conferences scheduled only when there is a problem	Time is not allocated for parent conferences. Conferences are viewed as only necessary when there is a problem to discuss.	Meet with the program director (if appropriate) to discuss the issue. At a staff meeting or workshop, discuss the benefits of parent conferences. Role-play ways to conduct a successful conference.

Resources for establishing the foundation

Allen, K.E., & Mantz, L. (1994). *Developmental profiles: Pre-birth through eight* (2d ed.). Albany, NY: Delmar.
  Presents an overview of development and the characteristics and milestones associated with each stage of development in all domains. Includes suggested activities to enhance development and developmental alerts.

Beaty, J.J. (1986). *Observing development of the young child.* Columbus, OH: Merrill.
  Focuses on observing six major aspects of development—social, emotional, physical, cognitive, language, and creative—in children ages 2 through 6 and includes a skills checklist.

Bellm, D., Whitehead, M., & Hnatiuk, P. (1997). *The early childhood mentoring curriculum, a handbook for mentors.* Washington, DC: National Center for the Early Childhood Work Force.

Reviews goals and principles of mentoring programs and provides strategies for developing mentoring skills, building strong and supportive mentoring relationships, and respecting diversity. Accompanied by a trainer's guide.

Bredekamp, S., & Copple, C. (Eds.). (1997). *Developmentally appropriate practice in early childhood programs* (rev. ed.). Washington, DC: NAEYC.
  Spells out the principles underlying developmentally appropriate practice and guidelines for classroom decisionmaking. Offers an overview of each period of development and extensive examples of practices appropriate and inappropriate with children of that age group.

Bredekamp, S., & Rosegrant, T. (Eds.). (1992). *Reaching potentials: Appropriate curriculum and assessment for young children, volume 1,* and (1995) *Reaching poten-*

tials: *Transforming early childhood curriculum assessment, volume 2.* Washington, DC: NAEYC.

Designed to assist early childhood professionals in applying the guidelines for appropriate curriculum content and assessment developed by NAEYC and NAESCS/SDE. Volume 1 addresses reaching developmental potentials for all children—including those with disabilities—and reaching the potentials of teachers and administrators. Volume 2 looks at the national standards in the fields of math, science, health, visual arts, music, social studies, physical education, and language and literacy.

Bronson, M.B. (1995). *The right stuff for children birth to 8: Selecting play materials to support development.* Washington, DC: NAEYC.

Describes the play materials that enhance children's motor, cognitive, and social-emotional development at each age and the key features to look for in each item.

Carter, M., & Curtis, D. (1996). *Reflecting children's lives: A handbook for planning child-centered curriculum.* St. Paul, MN: Redleaf.

This practical resource provides strategies for scheduling, observation, play, materials, space, and emergent themes. There are charts, assessment tools, and spaces for readers to record their observations. Planning for infants and toddlers is addressed in a separate chapter.

Cohen, D.H., Stern, V., & Balaban, N. (1983). *Observing and recording the behavior of young children* (3d ed.). New York: Teachers College Press.

Provides an excellent introduction to the purposes and techniques of observing young children in all areas of development.

Derman-Sparks, L., & the A.B.C. Task Force. (1989). *Anti-bias curriculum: Tools for empowering young children.* Washington, DC: NAEYC.

Contains many practical suggestions for helping adults understand how biases are unintentionally conveyed to children and how to minimize, deal with, and even eliminate those biases.

Diffily, D., & Morrison, K. (Eds.) (1996). *Family-friendly communication for early childhood programs.* Washington, DC: NAEYC.

Provides teachers with readable messages that they can use to communicate with parents and that can be tailored to particular programs or used as-is in newsletters, handouts, or other family communiques.

Dodge, D.T., Dombro, A.L., & Colker, L.J. (1998). *A journal for using "The Creative Curriculum for Infants and Toddlers."* Washington, DC: Teaching Strategies

Helps staff members to think about their own experiences, apply what they are learning, and reflect on their work. Each set of five books includes A Note for Trainers offering guidance on how to use the journal as the focus for ongoing staff development.

Dodge, D.T., & Phinney, J. (1990). *A parent's guide to early childhood education.* Washington, DC: Teaching Strategies.

Explains what happens in a developmentally appropriate early childhood program and the important role that parents play in supporting their child's learning. (English, Spanish, and Chinese editions.)

Feeney, S., Christensen, D., & Moravcik, E. (1990). *Who am I in the lives of children? An introduction to teaching young children* (4th ed.). Columbus, OH: Merrill.

Presents a variety of ways to work with young children to enhance self-concept, to enlarge the ability to make choices and clarify values, and to enhance learning; addresses CDA competencies in practical terms throughout each chapter.

Gonzalez-Mena, J. (1993). *Multicultural issues in child care.* Mountain View, CA: Mayfield.

Describes the importance of cultural competence for early childhood educators and encourages readers to increase their sensitivity to the child care practices of different cultures and enhance their communication skills so they can form effective partnerships with families.

Katz, L.G., & McClellan, D.E. (1997). *Fostering children's social competence: The teacher's role.* Washington, DC: NAEYC.

Suggests principles and strategies to guide teachers in strengthening children's social skills. Identifies well-intentioned practices very common in early childhood classrooms that actually undermine children's social competence.

Miller, K. (1985). *Ages and stages.* Marshfield, MA: Telshare.

A comprehensive guide to the stages children pass through as they develop physically, emotionally, and intellectually. Clear descriptions of children's behavior are accompanied by suggestions for how teachers can respond to meet children's needs and encourage their growth and development.

Neugebauer, B. (Ed.). (1992). *Alike and different: Exploring our humanity with young children* (rev. ed.). Washington, DC: NAEYC.

Each of the five chapters contains a series of articles on different aspects of children's self-image—bringing the world into your curricula; meeting the needs of all children; providing a diverse staff; learning from parents; and living in a changing world.

Weitzman, E. (1992). *Learning language and loving it.* Toronto: Hanen Centre.

Based on an on-site training program for early childhood staff, this book covers language learning from birth through the preschool years. Clear and vivid examples, illustrations, and graphics make the book practical and readable.

Training guides for the Head Start learning community _____

The following skill-based training guides include background information, workshop and coaching activities, handouts, suggested resources, and appendices. Each was published in cooperation with the Washington, DC-based Aspen Systems Corporation for the U.S. Department of Health and Human Services, Administration on Children, Youth and Families, and Head Start Bureau.

Colker, L.J. (1996). *Observation and recording: Tools for decision making.*

Koralek, D. (1998). *Emerging literacy: Linking social competence and learning.*

Koralek, D. (1998). *Individualizing: A plan for success.*

Koralek, D. (1996). *Enhancing children's growth and development.*

Available at no cost to all Head Start programs through the Head Start Publications Center, P.O. Box 26417, Alexandria, VA 22313-0417 (fax 703-683-5769). Other interested parties can purchase them at nominal cost from the U.S. Government Printing Office, Superintendent of Documents, Mail Stop: SSOP, Washington, DC 20402.

Further resources from NAEYC* _____

Abbott, C.F., & Gold, S. (1991). Conferring with parents when you're concerned that their child needs special services. *Young Children, 46*(4), 10-14.

Appropriate curriculum for young children: The role of the teacher [video]. (1988). Washington, DC: NAEYC. Depicts developmentally appropriate practices in programs for young children, illustrating the important role of the adult in helping children learn in a play-oriented environment and showing the adult's role in child-initiated activity.

Benham, N., Miller, T., & Kontos, S. (1988). Pinpointing staff training needs in child care centers. *Young Children, 43*(4), 9-16.

Bernat, V. (1993). Teaching peace. *Young Children, 48*(3), 36-39.

Bredekamp, S., & Willer, B. (1993). Professionalizing the field of early childhood education: Pros and cons. *Young Children, 48*(3), 82-84.

Brooke, G.E. (1994). My personal journey toward professionalism. *Young Children, 49*(6), 69-71.

Buckner, L.M. (1988). Viewpoint. On the fast track to . . . ? Is it early childhood education or early adulthood education? *Young Children, 43*(5), 5.

Burchby, M.M. (1992). A kindergarten teacher speaks to the governors—A story of effective advocacy. *Young Children, 47*(6), 40-43.

Chandler, P.A. (1994). *A place for me: Including children with special needs in early care and education settings.* Washington, DC: NAEYC. Gives staff strong encouragement and practical help to meet the challenges involved in making inclusion work.

Educating yourself about diverse cultural groups in our country by reading. (1993). *Young Children, 48*(3), 13-16.

Galinsky, E. (1988). Parents and teacher-caregivers: Sources of tension, sources of support. *Young Children, 43*(3), 4-12.

Green, M., & Widoff, E. (1990). Special needs child care: Training is a key issue. *Young Children, 45*(3), 60-61.

Jones, E. (Ed.). (1993). *Growing teachers: Partnerships in staff development.* Washington, DC: NAEYC.

Jones, E., & Nimmo, J. (1994). *Emergent curriculum.* Washington, DC: NAEYC. An inspiring, provocative staff development resource that listens in on the ongoing discussion of teachers as they go through a year "doing emergent curriculum."

Jorde Bloom, P. (1997). *A great place to work: Improving conditions for staff in young children's programs* (rev. ed.). Washington, DC: NAEYC.

Jorde Bloom, P. (1988). Teachers need "TLC" too. *Young Children, 43*(6), 4-8.

Morgan, E.L. (1989). Talking with parents when concerns come up. *Young Children, 44*(2), 52-56.

Passidomo, M. (1994). Moving from traditional to developmentally appropriate education: A work in progress. *Young Children, 49*(6), 75-78.

Sawyers, J.K., & Rogers, C.S. (1988). *Helping young children develop through play: A practical guide for parents, caregivers, and teachers.* Washington, DC: NAEYC.

Soto, L.D. (1991). Research in review. Understanding bilingual/bicultural young children. *Young Children, 46*(2), 30-36.

Stone, J. (1993). Caregiver and teacher language: Responsive or restrictive? *Young Children, 48*(4), 12-18.

Vartuli, S., & Fyfe, B. (1993). Teachers need developmentally appropriate practices too. *Young Children, 48*(4), 36-42.

_____

*To obtain a book published by NAEYC, call 800-424-2460 and ask for Resource Sales. For *Young Children* articles from the past five years, call the Institute for Scientific Information, 215-386-0100, ext. 5399, or fax 215-222-0840; from earlier issues, contact NAEYC's Public Affairs Department.

ESTABLISHING THE FOUNDATION

CHAPTER TWO

Infants

Developmentally appropriate infant rooms are warm and homelike to help children feel comfortable and secure. Caregivers meet infants' needs consistently, promptly, and lovingly in response to each child's individual schedule. Caregivers feed infants when the infants are hungry, change them when their diapers are wet or soiled, comfort them when they are distressed, and put them to sleep when they are tired. Caregivers hold and rock infants and allow them frequent opportunities to play on the floor or in a large, protected crawl area. Caregivers encourage infants to use their senses and their rapidly growing physical and cognitive skills to explore the environment. Weather permitting, each day infants and their caregivers go outdoors for fresh air and a change of scene.

This section offers information and guidance to help you oversee the environment, materials and equipment, program structure, activities and experiences, and supportive interactions of caregivers working with infants in center-based programs.

Some of the examples in this section refer to infants as *young* or *mobile.* These terms reflect the Child Development Associate (CDA) definitions of *young infants*– children from 0 to 8 months old– and *mobile infants*– children from 9 to 17 months old.

Environment

An appropriate environment for infants looks a lot like a home. There are spaces where caregivers can be with infants who need to be alone for a while; pictures hung at infant eye level; a variety of levels and textures; spaces for mobile infants to creep on, crawl in and out of, and walk around; and spaces set aside for young infants to safely play in without being hurt by the mobile infants. There is a place where parents and caregivers can communicate and share information about each child's daily routines and activities. The most important component of the environment in the infant room, however, is the caregiver, whose positive, supportive interactions help infants grow and develop. Following are examples of what you should see in a center-based program serving infants and why these arrangements of the environment are important.

Environment (cont'd)

What you should see	Why
patient, responsive caregivers who genuinely like caring for infants	Infants learn to trust the world by developing positive, caring relationships with the important adults in their lives. These adults include their parents and other family members, and caregivers in child development programs. When caregivers respond to children's needs promptly and consistently, infants learn that they are loved and valued. This is the foundation of trust and continued positive social development.
a safe, child-proofed setting, furnished with equipment that meets established safety standards	Infants learn about the world and develop skills through using their senses to explore their environment; thus, they need to be cared for in an environment that is free from safety hazards.
an area that welcomes parents to the room and encourages their involvement, including individual cubbies, a bulletin board, individual mailboxes (a shoe bag works well for this), or a similar system used by parents and caregivers to communicate about infants' special needs and to record information about each child's eating and diapering	Parents and caregivers are partners in the care of infants, and parents should be welcomed to the room. Parents like and need to know what their infants do during the day, so caregivers must keep good records. Although each infant has a primary caregiver, other caregivers also care for the child at one time or another; therefore, everyone needs to share information with parents. Moreover, parents might need to communicate important information about a child to all of the caregivers in the room.
many items that are commonly found in homes, such as hanging plants, carpeting, large floor pillows, pictures of infants' family members, and a rocking chair	Infants feel most secure at home with their parents. A homelike environment at the center helps infants feel secure and comfortable, which in turn contributes to their growth and development. It is also a more pleasant atmosphere for caregivers.
a well-organized, easy-to-clean diapering area, separated from the food-preparation area, with labeled shelves for supplies and with pictures, mirrors, or mobiles for the infants to look at	Diapering takes up a large part of the day, so this area needs to promote both caregiver efficiency and positive social interactions with infants. To ensure a healthy environment the area must be kept clean at all times. If supplies are stored conveniently, caregivers can relax and can use diapering times as opportunities to get to know and interact with individual infants. Pictures, mirrors, and mobiles can serve as stimuli for the caregivers' conversations with infants.

What you should see	**Why**
part of the floor covered with a hard, washable surface, such as linoleum	Mobile infants use a hard surface for their wheeled toys. Caregivers can serve meals here so that spilled food is easy to clean up. This area can also be used for sensory activities, such as water play or using playdough.
cribs located in an open area—arranged in a warm, noninstitutional way—where they are visible and accessible to caregivers; stackable "cuddle cots" used for older infants who nap less frequently	Most infants can sleep anywhere. Sleeping and other activities can take place in the same area, allowing caregivers to notice infants waking up so they can remove them from their cribs immediately. Infants thus spend less time in their cribs. Cuddle cots can be stacked, leaving more room for active play and exploration.
pictures (including photos of infants' families) and safety mirrors hung at infants' eye level	Pictures and mirrors need to be hung low enough on the walls for infants to see them without adult assistance. Family pictures help infants cope with being separated from their loved ones. Looking at themselves and others in a mirror can help infants begin to develop a sense of self.
low tables and chairs where infants can sit at mealtimes	Mobile infants enjoy feeding themselves. They can sit with their caregivers at the tables and eat together, family style.
a variety of safe spaces, including some that are carpeted and some at different levels	Infants need soft areas, such as carpeted floors, for learning to creep, crawl, and walk. Moving on different levels gives infants opportunities to see, touch, and hear their environment from different perspectives, which promotes their cognitive, social, and physical development.
an area in which young infants can play without being trampled by mobile infants	Young infants need protection from the mobile infants who are busy moving around the room. In an enclosed area, young infants can be safe but visible to the caregivers.
an outdoor play area that has space for infants to safely lie on a blanket or move about	Infants miss many kinds of experiences if they stay indoors all day. Outdoors they can breathe the fresh air, feel the wind, hear birds sing, touch the grass, or lie on a blanket in the shade and watch the sky.
low, open shelves stocked with a selection of toys, books, and other safe materials (two or three of each item)	Mobile infants can select the items they want to play with and can help put things away at cleanup time. Infants are not old enough to share, so having multiples of a few appropriate items is important.

When the environment is not working

During your visits to the infant room, observe what takes place in different areas of this caregiving setting. When you see that the environment is not promoting infants' growth and development, work with the caregivers to determine what changes are needed. Listed below are warning signs that the environment is inappropriate for infants, possible reasons caregivers might have for organizing the environment in these ways, and strategies you might try to improve the quality of the environment.

Warning signs	Why this might be happening	How you can help
mobile infants frequently trampling young infants in the play area	There is no safe area where young infants can play and explore out of the paths of the creepers, crawlers, and walkers.	Help caregivers rearrange the room to create a safe place for young infants to play on their blankets. Use soft blocks, gates, or low shelves to create a sheltered area.
pictures hanging at adult eye level, rather than at heights where infants can see them	Caregivers hang pictures where they can see them and don't realize that the infants can't see them, or the caregivers don't know that children can learn from looking at wall decorations.	Have caregivers get on the floor to view the room from infant eye level. Help move the pictures and other items to a level where infants can see them.
caregivers taking infants outdoors but keeping the children in their carriages and not letting them out to play and explore	Caregivers believe that the outdoor area is not safe for infants, or they don't understand that infants need to actively explore outdoors as well as indoors.	Go outdoors with the infants and caregivers and model ways to enjoy a number of outdoor activities.
a caregiver strapping an infant to a changing table, then walking across the room to gather diapering supplies	The caregiver thinks that the infant will remain safe while strapped to the changing table. The diapering supplies are stored in a different location instead of within reach of the changing area.	Explain that the straps might break or come undone, leaving the infant at risk. Have caregivers remove the straps so that they won't be tempted to use them in the future. Also, help caregivers move the diapering supplies within reach of the changing table.

Warning signs	Why this might be happening	How you can help
infants remaining in their cribs for a long time after waking up or remaining confined for long periods of time	Caregivers are busy meeting the needs of other infants and therefore believe that as long as an infant is safe, he or she can stay confined for a while with no ill effect. Cribs are in a separate area or are not easily visible from other parts of the room.	If necessary, help caregivers rearrange the room so that the cribs are located in open areas that are used for a variety of activities. Offer practical suggestions for addressing the needs of several infants at once. Suggest using a front pack to hold a young infant while diapering or reading a book to another child. Model ways to pay attention to more than one child at a time, such as holding a young infant while rolling a ball to a mobile infant.
all of the toys and play materials stored on high shelves where only adults can reach them	Caregivers want to control what the infants play with, think the infants will destroy the materials, or want to keep the room tidy at all times.	Help caregivers rearrange the room to allow the infants easy access to toys and play materials. If the shelves contain many materials, suggest that caregivers put away some of the materials, leaving duplicates of a few age-appropriate items on each shelf.
a room that seems cold and sterile, filled with objects and materials specifically designed for infant programs rather than items found in the average home	Caregivers don't realize the importance of a homelike environment in helping infants feel safe and comfortable while their parents are at work. They think that shiny new toys are a sign of a high-quality program.	Ask caregivers what would make the environment more like their own homes, and help them make the changes. Conduct training on how familiar household items, such as a set of mixing bowls, provide the same opportunities for learning as purchased toys, such as nesting cups.

Equipment and materials

Infant rooms generally provide care for infants of a wide range of ages and developmental stages. Because the equipment and materials needed for a 2-month-old are quite different from those needed for a 12-month-old (different items challenge infants who can hold things and those who cannot), the infant room must include materials and equipment that can meet the needs of infants at many different stages of development. As long as they are safe for infants to use, play materials can include homey items, such as pots and pans, or homemade toys, such as mobiles made by suspending plastic spoons from a hanger. Listed below are suggestions for what to include in child care settings for infants. The infant rooms in your center might not have all of the items listed, but you can share this list with caregivers and help them develop priorities based on the needs of each room.

Language development

- cloth or cardboard books—homemade or purchased—that are safe to mouth
- dishpan filled with pictures mounted on cardboard and covered with Contact® paper
- cloth or rubber puppets with no removable parts
- pictures of infants' families, familiar objects, and animals

Sensory stimulation

- mobiles—homemade or purchased
- mirrors (unbreakable)
- wall hangings (textured, touchable, and securely fastened)
- adult rocking chairs
- peek-a-boo toys
- Jack-in-the-box
- clutch balls
- rattles—homemade or purchased
- squeeze toys
- toys for sucking, chewing, and teething
- bell bracelets
- hand mitts made from baby socks
- beanbags
- cuddle toys, animals, and dolls

- push, pull, and squeeze toys
- music boxes (to wind up or to pull)
- tape or CD player and tapes or CDs
- texture balls
- texture glove made from a variety of materials (to be worn by an adult)
- water table or plastic bathtub or basin for water play
- plastic containers, cups, bowls, bottles, pitchers, and so on, for water play

Manipulative toys

- shape-sorting box
- pop-up toys
- large pop beads
- nesting boxes
- large, soft blocks
- large cardboard blocks
- containers in graduated sizes (such as plastic bowls or cups)
- pegboards with large holes and large, colored pegs
- large wooden stringing beads and short, thick strings or shoelaces
- cardboard boxes with lids
- busy boxes
- stacking post and rings

Developmentally appropriate infant rooms are warm and homelike to help children feel comfortable and secure. Caregivers meet infants' needs consistently, promptly, and lovingly in response to each child's individual schedule.

Gross-motor development

- small cars and trucks
- soft balls of various sizes
- riding toys (without pedals) propelled by arms or feet
- large cardboard boxes

Art

- large, nontoxic crayons and paper
- play dough and blunt, wooden dowels to use as tools
- box of small pieces of ribbons and fabrics of varied textures and colors
- fingerpaints and paper or shallow trays
- smocks (donated old shirts or plastic smocks)
- old tablecloth or plastic for floor covering

Dramatic play

- pots and pans
- large wooden or plastic spoons
- toy telephone
- hats
- purses and tote bags
- unbreakable tea set
- dolls (soft, unbreakable, washable, and multiethnic)

Outdoor play

- shallow wading pool
- water table or plastic bathtub or basin for sand or water play
- plastic containers, cups, bowls, bottles, pitchers (for sand or water play)
- strollers
- wagons and riding toys
- blankets to put down for young infants to lie on or crawl on
- umbrellas, screens, or "tents" to provide shade
- extra hats, mittens, and scarves for infants and caregivers
- balls
- large boxes
- small climbers

Equipment and materials (cont'd) _____

What you should see	**Why**
toys, materials, and equipment in good repair with no sharp edges, chipping paint, broken parts, or other hazards	Keeping infants safe is an important part of a caregiver's job. Caregivers should check everything in the room regularly and remove unsafe items.
a variety of safe, washable items (too large—including removable parts—for infants to swallow) that can be sucked, chewed, licked, squeezed, pinched, rolled, banged, or otherwise explored by infants	Using their senses to explore, infants put toys and other objects into their mouths to learn more about them. Teething infants also put things into their mouths because it feels good. Anything mouthed by infants should be washable. Germs spread quickly if the toys aren't disinfected daily. Choking is the number-one cause of accidental death for infants less than one year old, so all items in the room should be too big to be swallowed. Caregivers should examine the items to be sure that they meet the Consumer Product Safety Commission's recommendation that items available to infants should be no smaller than 1-5/8 inches in diameter.
household items (such as measuring cups, wooden spoons, bowls, and cardboard boxes) that infants can use as play materials	Household items help make the infant room more homelike, which helps infants feel secure.
materials (such as blocks and balls) that can be explored and used in numerous ways by infants at different stages of development	Infant rooms need open-ended materials that can be used in different ways by children of different ages and stages of development. Toys remain interesting to infants for a long time when they can use their growing skills to explore the items in new ways.
materials (such as telephones, dolls, small animals, puppets, and cooking utensils) that encourage mobile infants to engage in beginning levels of dramatic play	Dramatic play activities (such as rocking and feeding dolls, pretending to drink from cups, or stirring spoons around in pots) help mobile infants make sense of their world.
materials (such as large beads or blocks that fit together and can be taken apart, rattles, measuring cups, shape sorters, balls, and soft blocks) that respond to an infant's actions	By playing with toys and materials that respond when pulled, poked, banged, shaken, pushed, rolled, kicked, or hit, infants learn that their actions cause different things to happen—the basis for learning about cause-and-effect. These experiences help them feel that they have an effect on their environment.

What you should see	**Why**
materials (such as music boxes; tapes or CDs and a tape or CD player; chimes, a xylophone, and drums) that make music	Infants learn through using their senses, including hearing. Mobile infants enjoy moving to music, and they gradually learn the principle of cause-and-effect as they realize that music is coming from the record player or tape player, that turning the handle on the music box makes pleasing sounds, or that banging the drum in different ways makes distinct sounds.
materials (such as push-and-pull toys, riding toys, cars and trucks, and wagons) or rails that encourage infants to pull themselves up and move around the room or outdoors	Infants are born with little control over their movements, but they develop many physical skills during the first 17 months of life. As they interact with their environment in different ways, their motor development increases. These kinds of materials encourage infants to move around, to see more of the room or outdoor play area, and to become increasingly mobile.
materials (such as paper, large crayons, play dough, fingerpaints, scraps of material, and paste) to be used for creative art experiences	Art activities such as tearing paper or feeling the textures on scraps of material encourage mobile infants to use their senses, to be creative, to explore cause-and-effect, to do things for themselves, to develop an aesthetic sense, and to make things happen.
books (cloth or cardboard) with few or no words; illustrated by large, simple pictures of familiar objects, animals, and humans	Infants learn that books are exciting, important, and related to their lives. Reading books with infants stimulates their language development, helps them to connect words and images, and encourages them to develop a lifelong interest in books.
nonbreakable plates, bowls, and small cups, and child-size forks and spoons	Infants develop independence, self-esteem, and a great sense of accomplishment when they can do things for themselves. As soon as infants seem interested in feeding themselves, caregivers can provide finger foods and the necessary utensils.
large plastic trays or tables for sand and water play, and a variety of objects and tools that infants can use to explore these natural materials	Sand and water provide sensory experiences for infants. Playing with such materials promotes cognitive development as infants begin observing concepts, and the activity enhances language development as caregivers put these concepts into words.

When equipment and materials are inappropriate

Your periodic observations in the infant room allow you to identify signs that the materials and equipment are not facilitating growth and development. Infants develop and change quickly. A toy that was challenging last month might seem boring this month. A piece of equipment that was safe in the past soon becomes unsafe, as crawlers and walkers become more skilled at moving around the room. On the other hand, toys and materials that are too challenging will remain on the shelves or get tossed onto the floor. The following warning signs may let you know that caregivers need help to select appropriate materials for infants.

Warning signs	Why this might be happening	How you can help
loud music playing in the background all day	Caregivers are playing this music for their own pleasure.	Provide caregivers with suggestions of appropriate kinds of music to play for infants at certain times of the day, rather than all the time. Discuss which kinds of music are good for different activities or times of the day—soft, classical music is relaxing; music with a fast beat encourages infants to move.
infants seeming uninterested in the toys and materials available for their use	The toys and materials are one-dimensional, too simple, or too complex. Caregivers haven't noticed that the toys are not being used.	Hold a workshop on matching toys and materials to infants' stages of development. Provide household objects or discarded items that caregivers can use to make developmentally appropriate toys.
infants frequently fighting over some of the toys	Caregivers haven't noticed that these items are popular. Caregivers think that their role is to help infants learn to share rather than to provide multiples of popular toys.	Discuss the fact that learning to share is a developmental process that begins when infants feel a sense of ownership. Help caregivers observe to identify the most popular toys and materials so that multiples can be ordered.

Warning signs	Why this might be happening	How you can help
all of the books stored on high shelves where only adults can reach them	The books are made of paper that tears easily. Caregivers fear that without supervision infants could destroy the books.	Help caregivers display the books on a low shelf where infants can see and reach them. If the books are made of thin paper, sturdier books should be ordered. In the meantime, encourage caregivers to make books out of pictures of familiar objects and photographs covered with clear Contact paper. Pages of the picture books can also be covered with clear Contact paper.
the water play table used to store balls and other toys infants play with outdoors	Caregivers use this for storage because it gives them an excuse to not offer water play—they think that setting up the water play table for the infants is too much trouble or that infants should not get wet; or, no other place is available for storing the outdoor play items.	Ask caregivers if they need help finding appropriate storage sites for the materials kept in the water play table. If caregivers are still reluctant to offer water play, conduct a workshop in which some of the caregivers set up the water play table and others play at the table with plastic containers and other props. After about 10 minutes reverse the roles, allowing those who set up the table to have a turn playing. Then ask the first group to put away the equipment. Suggest that they ask their colleagues to help them. Lead a discussion about what infants gain from playing with water (and sand) and about how to include the infants in setting up and putting away the equipment.

Program structure: Schedule and routines

Infant rooms have flexible schedules so that caregivers can meet the individual needs of each child. Generally the schedule includes arrival periods, meal- and naptimes for the older infants, indoor and outdoor play times, and departure periods. Routines make up much of the infants' days and are, therefore, the most important events. Caregivers take advantage of routines—diapering, feeding, washing, and so on—to build relationships with infants and to promote their development in all areas.

What you should see	Why
a flexible schedule of simple and consistent routines that are altered to meet the needs of individual infants or to respond to "teachable moments"	Developmentally appropriate care for infants is based on meeting their individual sleeping and feeding schedules. This means that caregivers adjust to the infants' schedules, rather than expecting infants to adjust to the adults' schedules. Infants also benefit from their caregivers' responding to unplanned learning opportunities. For example, if a sudden snow flurry begins during outdoor time, caregivers can delay going back indoors so that the infants can watch the snow come down and melt and so they can feel the wet snow on their faces.
time included in the schedule for parents and caregivers to share information about infants	Parents and caregivers need time each day to share information about the infants' activities at home and at the center. Sharing helps the adults to provide consistent, effective care for the infant at home and at the center.
time in the schedule for infants and caregivers to go outdoors—ideally twice a day	Infants need fresh air and opportunities to experience the wind, grass, trees, singing birds, and other features of the outdoor environment. Going outdoors is also a refreshing and energizing change for caregivers.
sufficient time for infants to play alone or with others	Through play, infants discover how things work and how to make things happen. They also develop interests, make choices, and learn social skills.
caregivers talking and smiling with infants during routines like diapering or feeding and using these activities as opportunities to get to know each infant; adults using simple phrases to explain to the infants what they are doing	These are opportunities to build special relationships with infants, and thus to help infants develop trust and feel good about themselves. Infants learn about language when they are spoken to.

What you should see	Why
sufficient time for mobile infants to participate in routines and transitions	Mobile infants are capable of doing many things for themselves, but they may take longer than if someone does everything for them; for example, although a diaper change may take longer to complete, a child can hold the diaper until the caregiver is ready for it and can help wash and dry her own hands before being lifted down off the table.
caregivers removing infants from their cribs as soon as possible after they wake up	Infants need stimulation from the environment, which includes the adults who care for them and the other children in the room. This stimulation cannot take place if the infants are left alone in their cribs.
caregivers helping infants get down from the table or out of a high chair as soon as possible after mealtime	Sitting at the table can be confining, and infants should not be kept seated to keep them out of trouble. Infants need to be free to safely move and explore the room.
caregivers working as a team to meet the individual needs of the infants in the room	When a caregiver cannot respond immediately to an infant who needs assistance, a colleague should step in to help the infant. Staff members may serve as the primary caregivers for several infants; however, they also support their colleagues to make sure that children don't have to wait to be comforted.

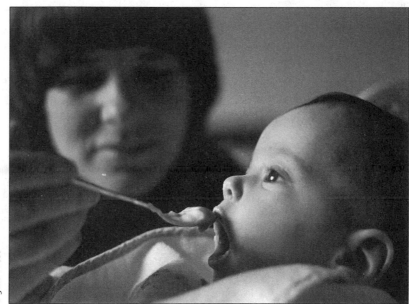

© Jim West

Sitting and waiting at a table or in a crib can be confining. Infants need to be free to safely move and explore the room.

When the program structure is not working

The following are a few of the warning signs that the program structure is not contributing to infants' growth and development. If you observe these or other warning signs, work with caregivers to analyze their daily schedule and their approaches to handling routines.

Warning signs	Why this might be happening	How you can help
every day in the infant room just like the one before, with little variation	The caregivers don't know how to balance infants' needs for consistency with infants' needs for challenging and stimulating new experiences.	Meet with the caregivers and discuss your observations. Talk about what parts of the schedule and which activities should remain consistent, and offer suggestions about when and how to include new activities.
mobile infants spending much of the day participating in caregiver-led activities	Caregivers think that infants learn only when they participate in structured activities, or caregivers are in a hurry to have infants grow up.	Reassure caregivers that infants have plenty of time to grow up. In the meantime caregivers can provide an interesting environment that allows children to make choices and control their own play.

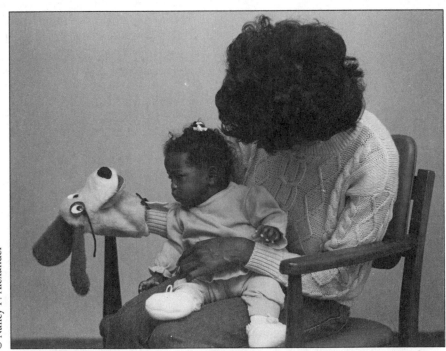

© Nancy P. Alexander

Some caregivers think that infants learn only when they participate in structured activities, or caregivers are in a hurry to have infants grow up.

Warning signs	Why this might be happening	How you can help
infants seeming uninvolved and passive; appearing bored and uninterested in the daily activities in the room	Caregivers are bored. They have stopped interacting with the infants or keep them confined in cribs, swings, or chairs.	Spend an hour or so video-taping in the infant room. View the videotape with the caregivers and discuss what the infants are doing or not doing. Point out opportunities for interactions and "teachable moments." Talk about ways to plan a more interesting day for both infants and caregivers.
caregivers rushing infants through diapering and other routines; one caregiver diapering all of the infants, one after another, while another caregiver plays with the children	Caregivers feel the need to hurry so as to get back to the other infants in their care, not realizing that routines such as diapering are excellent opportunities to get to know individual infants and to encourage older infants' independence. Or, perhaps, the caregiver doing the diapering prefers this task to playing with the children.	Model ways to interact with infants to help caregivers understand what infants are learning when they are talked to during routines like diaper changing. Observe the infant room at different times of the day to identify ways in which the caregivers do and do not work as a team. Share your observations and help caregivers learn how to support each other as they provide individualized care for the infants.
parents being rushed out of the infant room in the morning	The caregivers believe that the morning transition time is less stressful for infants if it is brief.	Help caregivers understand that infants and parents need the time to separate in a way that is comfortable for them. Explain that dealing with separation is a lifelong process. Ask them to think about times when they must separate from loved ones and how they handle their sad feelings.

Activities and experiences

When you visit the infant room, many different things are going on. Most of the infants are actively exploring their environment. They are crawling around the room, picking up toys and putting them into their mouths, climbing on pillows, pulling themselves up to stand, rolling balls, and so on. Young infants are likely to be sleeping, eating, or being held by caregivers. Listed below are examples of the activities and experiences you should see in infant rooms and explanations of why these examples are developmentally appropriate.

What you should see	Why
infants involved in a variety of different activities and experiences—some sleeping, some being fed, some playing by themselves, some playing with caregivers	Infant rooms typically include children at widely ranging ages and stages of development. Individual needs will not likely be met if all infants are doing the same things at the same times.
a caregiver placing a toy just beyond an infant's reach and talking to the infant as he tries to move forward and grasp the object	Challenges encourage infants to develop new skills. Caregivers, however, must observe infants and judge whether a particular challenge is appropriate or frustrating.
a caregiver taking several infants for a walk around the center, indoors and outdoors	Sometimes the infant room seems confining for both infants and caregivers. Walking around the center gives infants new perspectives and new experiences.
several young infants placed in a safe area where they look at and listen to what goes on in the room, look at themselves in a safety mirror, suck on their fists, watch a mobile, and so on	Young infants enjoy being part of the daily activities, but they need to be protected from the infants who are able to move around and might accidentally hurt them.
two or three mobile infants sitting at a low table fingerpainting on plastic trays or on oilcloth placed over the table	Creative-art activities such as fingerpainting provide opportunities for mobile infants to be with one or two other children, to explore and enjoy new materials, to make things happen, to develop fine-motor skills and creativity, and to use their senses to learn.
caregivers playing games with individual infants—peek-a-boo, rolling a ball, or filling and emptying a container	In addition to time spent on routines, each infant needs to spend one-on-one time with his or her caregiver every day. Individual attention helps infants gain a sense of security, which gives them the "courage" to try new things.

What you should see	**Why**
infants playing with materials that respond to their actions, such as jack-in-the-boxes, nesting cups, or playdough	Materials such as these help infants learn about concepts like cause-and-effect, means–end, or object permanence. They promote cognitive development and contribute to the infants' understanding of their world. Exploring such materials leads the infants to understand that they can affect what happens. They can make something appear and disappear, for example.
caregivers carrying young infants around the room and showing them different people and things in the environment	Young infants need a variety of stimulating experiences. Because they cannot yet move around the room by themselves, infants need adults to help them explore their surroundings.
caregivers describing to infants what they are playing with, what they are doing, or what is going on somewhere else in the room or outside	From many months of listening to caregivers and others talking to them, infants learn what language is, what words represent, and how to communicate with other humans.
caregivers and mobile infants working together to get ready to go outside	Older infants enjoy helping adults; it makes them feel appreciated and competent and allows them to develop self-help skills. Everyone needs to go outside to have a change of scenery, to play, and to get some fresh air.

© Michael Siluk

From many months of listening to caregivers and others talking to them, infants learn what language is, what words represent, and how to communicate with other humans.

When the activities are inappropriate

When you visit the infant room, you might not see the kinds of activities and interactions between caregivers and infants described earlier. The following warning signs should alert you to the possibility that infants are not engaged in developmentally appropriate activities.

Warning signs	Why this might be happening	How you can help
caregivers spending much of their time with the young infants, while the mobile infants wander around the room	The caregivers know that helping young infants feel safe and secure is important but don't know how to meet the needs of mobile infants.	Suggest that caregivers meet with you regularly to identify ways to challenge and stimulate the mobile infants. Visit the infant room and model ways to interact with a young infant while also playing with mobile infants.
infants being removed from activities that they are enjoying to participate in activities that the caregivers are conducting	The caregivers are excited about the activities that they have planned and think that the activities are good for the infants regardless of the infants' interests.	Remind the caregivers of the importance of respecting infants' needs and interests. Suggest that the adults remain flexible enough to conduct the planned activity on another day or to repeat it several times.
routines (diapering, feeding, and so on) being completed quickly and efficiently with little interaction between infants and caregivers	The caregivers see their duties as primarily custodial.	When you visit the infant room, model ways to use routines as opportunities to get to know individual infants, to teach them new skills, and to stimulate language development.
spending much of the day picking up toys, looking for lost belongings, cleaning up spills, and so on	The infant room is not well organized, and items are not stored where they are used. Caregivers are not aware that mobile infants can help perform some of the housekeeping activities.	Hold a brainstorming session with caregivers to identify ways to reorganize the room so that materials for children's use are stored on low, open shelves. Next, try to think of ways that mobile infants could participate in keeping the room in order; for example, mobile infants could put things back on low shelves, get their own coats off low hooks when it's time to go out, get the sponge from under the sink to clean up a spill, help to carry things outdoors or back indoors, and so on. Be sure that caregivers understand that infants enjoy helping and that their participation enhances their independence and self-esteem.

Suggest that caregivers meet with you regularly to identify ways to challenge and stimulate the mobile infants.
Visit the infant room and model ways to interact with a young infant while also playing with mobile infants.

Supportive interactions

Because caregivers are the most important component of the environment in the infant room, their interactions with infants are crucial to providing high-quality care. Infants learn basic trust as they develop warm, secure relationships with the important adults in their lives. This sense of trust fosters infants' development and encourages them to learn new skills. Look for the following kinds of interactions when you visit the infant room.

What you should see	Why
caregivers responding immediately to crying infants, trying to determine the reason for children's discomfort, and attempting to help distressed infants feel better	Infants need to develop a sense of trust. When adults respond quickly to their cries of distress and try to find out what is needed, infants learn to feel secure and to trust the persons who care for them.
caregivers sitting on the floor with infants and reading books, singing songs, holding young infants, and so on	Interactions with infants are most effective when caregivers get down to the infants' level and maintain frequent eye contact with them.
caregivers holding young infants close, looking into their faces, smiling, and talking to them	Young infants are learning to recognize the important adults in their lives. Close physical contact helps infants develop attachments to these adults, which contributes to their sense of security. Through eye contact and smiling, infants learn about communicating with others.
caregivers asking mobile infants to help clear the dishes from the table	Infants learn prosocial behaviors, such as being helpful, when caregivers provide opportunities for the children to carry things outside, help clean up, look for lost toys, and so on. These activities are enjoyable and contribute to the development of positive self-concepts.
a caregiver recognizing an infant's fear of strangers and comforting the frightened child	At 9 to 12 months, and again at 17 to 18 months, an infant might become anxious in the presence of strangers. Caregivers must recognize this stage as part of normal development, provide comfort and support, and help the infant get used to being with new people.
a caregiver showing pleasure and praising an infant who has pulled herself up to standing	Caregivers' praise and approval let infants know that their skills and accomplishments are recognized as important. Infants then feel encouraged to continue developing and learning new skills.
a caregiver welcoming a nursing mother and placing the infant in her mother's arms	Nursing mothers feel supported when caregivers graciously share the care of infants and ease the infant's transition from their care to the mother's.

34

What you should see	**Why**
caregivers responding to infants' attempts at communication—gestures, first words, cries, and so on, by "talking" back	When caregivers respond to their sounds and gestures, infants learn about the give-and-take of communicating with others. This encourages them to continue trying to let others know their needs and thoughts.
caregivers demonstrating desirable social behaviors that infants can imitate	Infants learn from observing and interacting with everything in their environment. They learn social behaviors, both desirable and undesirable, by participating in relationships with adults and then imitating the adults' behaviors.
caregivers encouraging mobile infants to take off their own shoes as they get ready for naptime	Mobile infants want and need to feel competent. They are able to perform many tasks and should be allowed to do so as often as possible; for example, they can feed themselves, pull off their socks, hang their coats on low hooks, and so on.
caregivers encouraging mobile infants to explore the environment	When caregivers have set up a safe environment, mobile infants are free to explore without being told to.
a caregiver remaining calm and positive when a mobile infant refuses a request to drink her juice	As mobile infants begin to master their environment and move out into the world, they develop the desire to become independent. Uncooperative behavior may be a sign that they need to learn to do things for themselves. Caregivers should respond to this need for greater independence by allowing infants to do many things for themselves.
caregivers showing mobile infants how to pretend to feed a baby or talk on the telephone	One of the ways children learn to make sense of their world is through dramatic play. Sometimes caregivers need to get children started on dramatic play by showing them how to use a prop. Imitating adult activities helps infants to express their feelings and to understand the world around them.
caregivers offering mobile infants simple choices: "Do you want to use the wagon or the lawn mower?"	The ultimate goal of positive guidance is to help children develop self-discipline. Positive guidance techniques, such as setting limits, redirecting behavior, and providing choices, help infants learn what the limits are to their behavior.

When interactions are inappropriate

As you observe in the infant room, you might see the following warning signs or other indications of problems. When you observe warning signs, respond immediately with strategies to improve the interactions between adults and infants.

Warning signs	Why this might be happening	How you can help
a caregiver making fun of an infant having difficulty picking up a piece of finger food	The caregivers do not know the importance of showing respect for infants' efforts. Caregivers think that infants don't know what the caregivers are laughing about.	Discuss with the caregivers how they approach learning a new task and ask them what kind of encouragement helps them to continue their efforts when they feel frustrated. Remind them that while humor may be helpful in some situations, making fun of anybody is demeaning. Explain that infants may not understand words, but they are learning from everything they see and hear in their environment.
a caregiver putting an infant in a crib after she pulls another child's hair	The caregiver is overly concerned about keeping infants safe or thinks that infants will learn to behave appropriately if they are punished by being placed in cribs or other confining equipment.	Conduct a workshop on the difference between punishment and discipline and using positive guidance techniques to help infants learn self-discipline. Role-play a more helpful way to respond to such behavior in the future.
caregivers not interacting or communicating with one another	The caregivers have had few opportunities to get to know each other and, therefore, don't know how to work as a team; or the caregivers are so busy attending to their duties that they have no time to socialize with each other.	Ask caregivers to complete a task or a training activity together to promote team building. Hold a social event—Sunday-morning brunch, for example—at which you get to know each other without talking about infants or the center.
caregivers telling infants to stop behaviors, such as crying, dropping things on the floor, or putting everything in their mouths	Caregivers have inappropriate expectations for infants' behavior because they do not understand the development stages infants pass through. They think that infants can control their own behavior.	Meet with caregivers to review the stages of infant development and the typical behaviors that adults may find annoying but are signs that infants are developing normally.

Warning signs	Why this might be happening	How you can help
caregivers lining up infants in highchairs or carrying seats at mealtime and silently feeding the children	Caregivers find feeding all of the infants according to the same schedule to be most efficient because caregivers only have to clean up once. They do not realize that feeding time is an opportunity to talk and get to know individual children.	Model for caregivers how to use mealtimes as opportunities for interacting with infants and for promoting their development. Remind caregivers that infants need to eat according to individual schedules.
caregivers leaving crying infants in their cribs or other confined areas for relatively long periods of time	Caregivers don't know how to help a particular infant feel more comfortable. They have only one way of responding to crying infants, and if that approach does not work, they don't know what else to do.	Suggest that caregivers ask parents what works to calm their crying infants. They can also observe the techniques that their colleagues use to help crying infants feel better. Help caregivers understand that each infant is an individual with a unique temperament. What soothes one infant may not calm another.
caregivers conversing with each other much of the time, rather than talking to infants	Caregivers feel embarrassed talking to infants or do not realize that infants learn to communicate when other humans talk or sing to them.	Remind caregivers that when infants are spoken to, they are likely to coo and gurgle in response. Coos and gurgles are the beginning of communication. Model such interactions when you visit the infant room.
a caregiver grabbing a toy from an infant and screaming, "Leave those pop beads alone. André was playing with them first."	The caregiver might be feeling a high level of stress, perhaps because she does not have realistic expectations for infants' behavior and does not know how use positive guidance techniques.	Intervene as quickly as possible so that the caregiver can regain composure. Then, in a private meeting explain that this kind of behavior is not acceptable because it can be damaging to children. Offer to help the caregiver learn about infant development, positive guidance techniques, and healthy ways to handle stress. Check in with this caregiver periodically to see if she or he is developing the skills needed to support infants' development. In extreme cases, if there is no improvement in the caregiver's behavior, you may have to suggest that the caregiver pursue a different career.

Resources for working in infant rooms

Carnegie Task Force on Meeting the Needs of Young Children. (1994). *Starting Points: Meeting the needs of our youngest children.* New York: Carnegie Task Force on Meeting the Needs of Young Children. (Available through NAEYC.)

Documents the "quiet crisis" affecting millions of children under age 3 and their families.

Dodge, D.T., Dombro, A.L., & Colker, L.J. (1998). *A parent's guide to infant/toddler programs.* Washington, DC: Teaching Strategies.

Shows parents how warm and responsive care—at home and in child care—helps shape the future development of infants and toddlers and their ability to learn. It outlines what and how children learn during these crucial years and suggests ways that caregivers/teachers and parents can work together. (English and Spanish editions.)

Dodge, D.T., Dombro, A.L., & Koralek, D.G. (1992). *Caring for infants and toddlers* (Vols. 1 and 2). Washington, DC: Teaching Strategies.

A comprehensive, self-instructional training program in two volumes that covers the CDA Functional Areas. A trainer's guide is also available.

Dombro, A.L., & Bryan, P. (1991). *Sharing the caring.* New York: Simon & Schuster.

Parents and teachers are encouraged to be aware of their feelings about sharing the care of infants and toddlers. The authors offer practical suggestions of ways to build partnerships that will help children feel safe and secure in child care.

Dombro, A.L., Colker, L.J., & Dodge, D.T. (1997). *The creative curriculum for infants and toddlers.* Washington, DC: Teaching Strategies.

Provides a comprehensive yet easy-to-use framework for planning and implementing a developmentally appropriate program for infants and toddlers in a center-based or family child care setting. Accompanied by a journal for caregivers/teachers implementing the curriculum.

Dombro, A.L., & Wallach, L. (1988). *The ordinary is extraordinary: How children under three learn.* New York: Simon & Schuster.

A look at the world through the eyes of infants and toddlers. Readers see how children learn physical, cognitive, emotional, and social skills by participating in daily routines with their parents and teachers.

Gonzalez-Mena, J., & Widmeyer, D.E. (1997). *Infants, toddlers, and caregivers.* Palo Alto, CA: Mayfield.

An insightful look at life in a child care setting. In addition to learning about who children are at different ages, teachers will come to appreciate that there is nothing more important than their relationship with the infants and toddlers they care for.

Greenman, J., & Stonehouse, A. (1996). *Prime times: A handbook for excellence in infant and toddler programs.* St. Paul, MN: Redleaf.

Explains the needs of infants and toddlers and of their families and caregivers and describes ways to use this information to provide quality programs.

Jalongo, M.R. (1988). *Young children and picture books: Literature from infancy to six.* Washington, DC: NAEYC.

An excellent book for teachers on what constitutes high-quality literature and art for young children and how children benefit from good books.

Lally, J.R., Griffin, A., Fenichel, E., Segal, M., Szanton, E., & Weissbourd, B. (1995). *Caring for infants and toddlers in groups: Developmentally appropriate practice.* Washington, DC: Zero to Three.

Defines specialized knowledge and skills and program features that support the development of infants and toddlers.

Weitzman, E. (1992). *Learning language and loving it.* Toronto: Hanen Centre.

Based on an on-site training program for early childhood staff, this book covers language learning from birth through the preschool years. Clear and vivid examples, illustrations, and graphics make the book practical and readable.

Wilson, L.C. (1995). *Infants and toddlers, curriculum and teaching.* Albany, NY: Delmar.

This comprehensive guide to caring for infants and toddlers is an excellent resource for teachers. Part 3, "Matching Caregiver Strategies and Child Development," is a particularly useful source of information on child development and developmentally appropriate practice.

Audiovisual resource

Colker, L.J. (1995). *Observing young children: Learning to look, looking to learn.* Washington, DC: Teaching Strategies.

This 30-minute videotape with accompanying user's guide trains staff and providers on how to objectively and accurately observe children. Promotes skills in focusing observations to learn more about children, to measure children's progress, and to evaluate the effectiveness of their program.

Further resources from NAEYC*

Balaban, N. (1992). The role of the child care professional in caring for infants, toddlers, and their families. *Young Children, 47*(5), 66-71.

Daniel, J.E. (1993). Infants to toddlers: Qualities of effective transitions. *Young Children, 48*(6), 43-46.

Godwin, A., & Schrag, L. (1988). *Setting up for infant care: Guidelines for centers and family day care homes.* Washington, DC: NAEYC.
Explains in plain English how to work with parents, keep children safe and healthy, and help children develop emotionally, socially, and cognitively.

Gonzalez-Mena, J. (1992). Taking a culturally sensitive approach in infant-toddler programs. *Young Children, 47*(2), 4-9.

Greenberg, P. (1987). Ideas that work with young children. What is curriculum for infants in family day care (or elsewhere)? *Young Children, 42*(5), 58-62.

Highberger, R., & Boynton, M. (1983). Preventing illness in infant/toddler day care. *Young Children, 38*(3), 3-8.
What are the most effective prevention techniques; basic, simple precautions; sanitation checklist.

Honig, A.S. (1993). Mental health for babies: What do theory and research teach us? *Young Children, 48*(3), 69-76.

Hughes, F.P., Elicker, J., & Veen, L.C. (1995). A program of play for infants and their caregivers. *Young Children, 50*(2), 52-58.

Meyerhoff, M.K. (1994). Viewpoint. Of baseball and babies: Are you unconsciously discouraging father involvement in infant care? *Young Children, 49*(4), 17-19.

Pizzo, P.D. (1990). Family-centered Head Start for infants and toddlers: A renewed direction for Project Head Start. *Young Children, 45*(6), 30-35.

Ross, H.W. (1992). Integrating infants with disabilities? Can "ordinary" caregivers do it? *Young Children, 47*(3), 65-71.

---

*To obtain a book published by NAEYC, call 800-424-2460 and ask for Resource Sales. For *Young Children* articles from the past five years, call the Institute for Scientific Information, 215-386-0100, ext. 5399, or fax 215-222-0840; from earlier issues, contact NAEYC's Public Affairs Department.

CHAPTER THREE

Toddlers

An appropriate program for toddlers (18 months to 3 years) provides a balance between a toddler's conflicting needs for security and independence. Caregivers respond to toddlers' struggles to become independent by allowing them to make simple choices and to do things for themselves. Caregivers comfort children who are distressed and provide support as toddlers attempt new tasks. Children do many of the same things that they do at home with their parents, and, because most toddlers are very active, they have opportunities to climb, run, crawl, and move around. This section offers information and guidance to help you oversee the environment, materials and equipment, program structure, activities and experiences, and supportive interactions of caregivers working with toddlers in center-based programs.

Environment

An appropriate environment for toddlers includes several small, clearly defined interest areas where two or three toddlers can engage in activities such as playing with water or sand, finger-painting, building with large cardboard blocks, or dancing to music. There are multiples of popular toys and materials so that children do not have to wait too long to use their favorite items. To foster toddlers' independence, materials are displayed so that the children can select what they would like to use and can put things away at cleanup time. Caregivers have arranged the furniture and equipment so that toddlers have plenty of room to move about and use their large muscles. To ensure smooth, safe operations, the toddler room is set up so that caregivers can see what is happening in all parts of the room. Parents feel welcome in the toddler room; there is an area set aside for parent-caregiver communications. Listed below are examples of what you should see in a center-based program serving toddlers and why these arrangements of the environment are important.

Environment (cont'd)

What you should see	Why
a few simple interest areas, stocked with a variety of age-appropriate toys and materials	When a varied and interesting environment is set up for toddlers, they can exercise their growing independence by deciding what they want to do and with whom they want to play.
an art and sensory area with a washable floor (ideally with a drain), equipped so that easel painting and sand and water play can be offered daily	Toddlers are ready to paint at easels with "fat" brushes and a few colors of paint. Painting promotes motor development, encourages creativity, and builds self-esteem. Sand and water play is soothing, encourages exploration, and helps toddlers learn about principles such as cause-and-effect. Caregivers are more likely to offer these "messy" activities daily if the floor is washable.
a well-organized, easy-to-clean diapering area, separated from the food-service area and the main activities of the room, and pediatric-size toilets and sinks	Most young toddlers still wear diapers. Typically, older toddlers are ready for toilet learning around age two; boys commonly start later, however. Children who are already, or are becoming, toilet trained need easy access to pediatric-size toilets and sinks that they can use without adult assistance.
low, open shelves, stocked with toys and other materials and labeled with pictures to indicate where the toys are stored	Toddlers are trying hard to be independent and to feel competent. Low, open shelves allow them to select and replace play materials without asking adults for assistance. Labels let toddlers know where the materials are stored.
personal places (such as lofts or large cardboard boxes lined with blankets or pillows) that are visible to teachers	At times, when the noise and activity levels in the toddler room are overwhelming, some toddlers like refuge from the noise and activities to recoup their energy or just to be alone. Personal places allow toddlers to be alone or to observe—from a distance—what is going on in the room. These spaces must be visible so that caregivers can supervise all of the children in the room.
large, open spaces and spaces containing ramps, steps, and other equipment that encourage physical activity	Fast-growing toddlers tend to be energetic. They need many opportunities to use their gross-motor skills. Because they cannot confine their running, jumping, climbing, and related activities to outdoor play periods, they need indoor space and equipment that facilitates active play.
an area that welcomes parents to the room, encourages them to communicate with caregivers, offers information about the toddlers' activities at the center, and shares parenting resources	Parents and caregivers need to support each other as they respond to toddlers' conflicting needs to be independent and to stay in close touch with familiar people and experiences. Daily interactions help all the adults plan an appropriate program that meets individual needs. Most parents are eager to learn about toddler development and effective parenting techniques.

What you should see	**Why**
pictures showing familiar objects, animals, and people (including the toddlers' families), hung at the toddlers' eye level	Toddlers cannot see pictures hung at adult eye level. Displaying pictures of familiar objects, animals, and people helps toddlers feel secure.
a safe outdoor play area containing low swings, climbing structures, and other equipment sized for toddlers	In many playgrounds the equipment is sized for preschoolers or school-age children and therefore is unsafe for toddlers: rungs on ladders are too far apart, swings are too high, slides are too tall, and so on. Equipment sized for toddlers will provide challenges for them and will allow toddlers to master skills without getting hurt.
a separate cubby or other private storage space for each toddler in the room	Toddlers may spend many hours at the center, so they must feel safe and secure there. They can store personal items, including special blankets or stuffed animals from home in private cubbies. Being able to bring special items and having spaces to store things that are not to be shared, either for sanitary reasons or because toddlers are not ready to share these items, makes toddlers feel at home at the center.

© Mary K. Gallagher

An appropriate setting for toddlers has a few simple interest areas, stocked with a variety of age-appropriate toys and materials; has an art and sensory area for daily use; and has personal areas that are visible to teachers.

When the environment is not working

Maintaining an environment that meets the needs of all the toddlers in the room is not easy. As you regularly observe in the toddler room, you may see children fighting over favorite toys, running around the room, or clambering for a caregiver's attention because they need adult assistance to reach the toys. These behaviors may be clues that the environment is not effectively promoting the toddlers' development. Listed below are warning signs that the environment is inappropriate for toddlers, possible reasons that caregivers might have for organizing the environment in these ways, and strategies you might try to improve the quality of the environment.

Warning signs	Why this might be happening	How you can help
a caregiver saying, "No," to toddlers who are climbing on the tables or other pieces of furniture	The room doesn't have enough places or equipment for toddlers to safely use their gross-motor skills.	Ask caregivers to make a list of all of the ways children can use gross-motor skills in the classroom and outdoors. If the list seems too short, help caregivers think of new ways to offer opportunities for active play.
toddlers falling off the climbing equipment or pinching their fingers in the kitchen cupboards	The equipment that toddlers are using was designed and sized for use by preschoolers and is therefore unsafe for toddlers.	Work with caregivers to develop a safety checklist that they can use to regularly assess classroom safety. Explain the importance of using equipment designed for toddlers or, if necessary, adapting preschoolers' equipment to make it safe for toddlers. Caregivers could, for example, take the doors off the cupboards.
toddlers fighting over favorite toys	Caregivers are trying to teach toddlers to share, rather than providing multiples of favorite items.	Make a chart showing the developmental steps involved in learning to share, beginning with feeling a sense of ownership. Use the chart to explain to caregivers that learning to share is a developmental process. Toddlers will learn to share in time. Observe in the toddler room to see which toys and materials are most in demand, then order multiples of these items.

Warning signs	Why this might be happening	How you can help
most of the toys and materials stored on high shelves out of toddlers' reach	Caregivers want to keep the room neat or fear that the toddlers will misuse the toys without adult supervision.	Explain to caregivers that, if the toys are stored on labeled shelves where toddlers can reach them, the toddlers can learn to put things away, which will foster their independence. Help caregivers arrange the materials and label the shelves appropriately.
toddlers seeming frustrated, getting into disagreements, and crying easily	Caregivers have not provided personal spaces where toddlers can take a break from the group. They fear that toddlers won't be safe if they are alone, or caregivers don't understand that sometimes toddlers need to "get away" for a while.	Suggest ways to provide safe places—such as large, open boxes lined with pillows— that allow toddlers to feel removed from the rest of the group but remain visible to the caregivers. Explain that because toddlers are learning many new tasks quickly, they become easily frustrated.
toddlers running around a lot and rarely playing with the toys and materials; the toddler room arranged with one large, open space, and all toys and equipment stored on shelves against the walls	Caregivers are trying to accommodate the toddlers' needs for a safe place to run, jump, and engage in other energetic pursuits.	Help caregivers draw sample floor plans that show ways to rearrange the room to create a few interest areas, stocked with items of interest to toddlers. Help caregivers move the furniture and equipment so that they can put their plans into action. Observe in the classroom so you can give caregivers examples of how the new arrangement is helping toddlers grow and learn.
toddlers asking caregivers to help them find the things they want to use, for example, paper to go with the crayons or blankets that go with the dolls	Materials that are used together (such as paper and crayons) are kept on different shelves, not next to each other. Caregivers don't understand that toddlers are more likely to use materials appropriately when items that are used together are stored together.	Ask the caregivers to categorize the toys and materials in their room. Groupings might include art, dramatic play, music, blocks, books, and so on. Help the caregivers decide how and where to store the items that go together.

When the environment is not working (cont'd)

Warning signs	Why this might be happening	How you can help
some interest areas seldom used by the children	Caregivers don't realize how quickly toddlers' interests grow and change; therefore, caregivers seldom change the materials provided in the interest areas; or the interest areas aren't appropriate for toddlers.	Provide a workshop or one-on-one sessions on how to observe children's behavior and how to use observation notes as a source of valuable information about toddlers' changing skills and interests.

Equipment and materials

Toddler classrooms contain equipment and materials that are appropriate for a wide span of ages and developmental stages, usually 18 months to 3 years. The toys and materials are ones that can be used in many different ways and with little adult assistance, including push and pull toys, climbing equipment, and items that encourage all types of gross-motor development. The materials are varied to allow toddlers to practice their new cognitive, physical, and social skills. Listed below are suggestions for what to include in each interest area of a toddler classroom. The toddler rooms in your center may not have all of the items listed, but you can share this list with the caregivers and help them develop priorities based on the needs of each room.

Language development

- homemade or purchased simple books about
  - feelings and attitudes
  - families and friends
  - everyday living experiences
  - science and nature
  - fun and fantasy
- rocking chair, soft chair, mattress, pillows
- carpeted floor
- cloth puppets
- pictures of toddlers' families, familiar objects, and animals

Music

- tape or CD player and tapes or CDs
- rhythm instruments (with no sharp edges)

Blocks

- large, soft blocks
- large cardboard blocks
- hollow blocks
- small cars and trucks
- animal props (farm and/or zoo animals)
- people props: multiethnic family sets and community helpers

Gross-motor development

- cars and trucks
- soft balls of various sizes
- riding toys (without pedals) propelled by arms or feet
- large cardboard boxes
- wagons

Manipulative toys

- shape-sorting box
- puzzles with a few large pieces
- Legos® (largest size)
- pop-up toys
- large pop beads

Equipment and materials (cont'd)

- nesting boxes
- stacking rings
- containers in graduated sizes (such as plastic bowls or cups)
- pegboards with large holes and large, colored pegs
- large, wooden stringing beads and short, thick strings or shoelaces
- plastic pop beads
- cardboard boxes with lids
- mirrors (unbreakable)
- beanbags and baskets to toss them into
- push and pull toys

Art

- old tablecloth or plastic for floor covering

- smocks (donated old shirts or plastic smocks)
- easels
- paints
- brushes
- newsprint
- large nontoxic crayons and paper
- felt-tip markers
- white and colored chalk
- playdough and utensils
- fingerpaints and paper
- shallow trays for fingerpainting

Dramatic play

- pots and pans
- stuffed animals
- dolls

- toy telephones
- hats
- purses and tote bags
- unbreakable tea sets
- dolls (soft, unbreakable, washable, and multiethnic)
- doll beds
- doll carriages

Outdoor play

- water table or plastic bathtub or basin (for sand or water play)
- plastic containers, cups, bowls, bottles, pitchers (for sand and water play)
- wagons and riding toys
- balls
- large boxes
- small climbers

© Jeffrey High Image Productions

Large, open spaces and spaces containing ramps, steps, and other equipment that encourage physical activity are essential. A safe outdoor play area with equipment sized for toddlers is equally important.

Equipment and materials (cont'd) _____

What you should see	Why
materials (such as beanbags, empty spools, and small blocks) and containers (such as baskets, boxes, and buckets) that toddlers can use for filling and dumping	Filling containers and then dumping the contents is a favorite toddler activity, not because it annoys adults, but because it helps toddlers learn about space and volume and gives them a sense of control over their environment. Also, children learn through repeated success.
materials (such as playdough and utensils, easels, paper, crayons, paints, brushes, and paste) for creative expression	Most toddlers are not interested in creating products, however they enjoy using their senses to explore the properties of materials such as playdough. They also feel a sense of control—the ability to make something happen—as they spread paint on paper or paste scraps of fabric to a piece of paper.
wheeled toys (such as wagons, scooters, and trucks) that can be ridden, pushed, or pulled	Toddlers love to move, and wheeled toys allow them to use their gross-motor skills to propel themselves around the room or playground. Most toddlers do not have the physical skills needed to pedal tricycles.
sand and water tables and accessories (such as pitchers, cups, funnels, scoops, and spoons)	Sand and water are natural materials that appeal to toddlers' senses of touch, sight, and sound. Playing with sand and water is soothing and allows toddlers to experiment and develop their fine-motor skills, eye-hand coordination, and cognitive skills.
picture books about familiar activities or experiences that depict many different ethnic groups	Books stimulate the development of language skills and set the stage for children's later interest in reading. Caregivers can read to individual children or to small groups, or toddlers can look at books by themselves.
large, soft blocks and accessories (such as small animals, people, and transportation toys)	Toddlers use blocks to build, sort, pretend, and practice their fine- and gross-motor skills. Accessories stimulate different kinds of imaginative play.
large, hollow blocks that are not heavy	Toddlers feel competent and in control as they carry blocks around the room. Some older toddlers might also use the blocks to build roads, houses, or other simple structures.

What you should see	**Why**
manipulatives (such as big wooden beads and strings or large Legos) and puzzles with only a few pieces	Manipulatives must be sized appropriately for toddlers. As they develop fine-motor and cognitive skills, toddlers learn to use these materials. Once they master a task—such as threading beads on a string—they are likely to want to practice it again and again.
materials (such as music boxes, tapes and CDs, a tape or CD player, and rhythm instruments) for listening to or making music	With these pieces of equipment on hand, caregivers and toddlers can play many different kinds of music. Toddlers love to move to music, play along with their own rhythm instruments, and sing songs. Several brands of tape players are designed for use by toddlers, who can use them to record their own music or conversations.
equipment (such as climbers, a rocking boat, and an old mattress) for use in gross-motor activities (such as climbing, sliding, rocking, or jumping)	Most toddlers are constantly on the move as they use their whole bodies to learn. Participating in physical activities allows toddlers to develop new motor skills and to feel control over their environment.
dramatic play items (such as clothes, hats, dolls, mirrors, puppets, and a variety of props related to specific themes)	Toddlers' imaginative play, alone or with a few other children, is about real experiences that they have observed or participated in at home or at the center. Their dramatic play usually focuses on events like cooking, cleaning, leaving and returning home, caring for babies, or driving a car. Dramatic play helps toddlers understand life and helps them learn to play with others.
personal items (such as blankets, stuffed animals, and coats) that belong to each toddler and household items (such as soft cushions, carpeted areas, plants, and a rocking chair) that make the room seem more like home	Toddlers feel most secure at home with their parents. The toddler room feels more like home if it includes toddlers' personal belongings and other items that are like those found at home—pots and pans, pictures of toddlers' families, curtains, and soft lighting.

When equipment and materials are inappropriate

Your regular observations in the toddler room allow you to identify warning signs that the materials and equipment are not helping the toddlers grow and develop. The inappropriate materials and equipment might also be making it difficult for caregivers to enjoy caring for toddlers. If you observe the following warning signs or other indications of problems, help caregivers to make the necessary adjustments to ensure that the toddler room contains developmentally appropriate materials and equipment.

Warning signs	Why this might be happening	How you can help
toddlers becoming cranky while waiting for adults to help them use materials	Caregivers have not provided sufficient materials and activities that toddlers can use without adult assistance. Caregivers do not understand that toddlers are capable of doing many things for themselves.	Ask caregivers to list all of the materials in the room, dividing them into the following categories: *children can use these with no adult assistance* and *children need adult assistance to use these*. If more materials fall into the first category than into the second, help caregivers select new materials that toddlers can use independently.
dolls, books, and pictures in the toddler room that do not reflect the ethnic groups of the toddlers in the room	Caregivers have not considered this an important factor when selecting materials for the room or they are using the materials already in the room without giving thought to antibias issues.	Offer a workshop or provide materials on how culturally sensitive play materials contribute to children's developing sense of self. Include information about how to assess equipment and materials in the room to make sure that they reflect different ethnic groups, and supply information on where to obtain appropriate materials.
multiples of some toys sitting on the shelves; toddlers fighting over other toys, for which there are no multiples	Caregivers don't know which toys are popular and which are not.	Have caregivers put away the less-popular toys temporarily; the toddlers might find these toys interesting after they have been out of sight for a while. Order more of the popular items. Have caregivers set up a schedule for periodically reviewing their observation notes to assess the popularity of the equipment and materials in their room.

Help teachers understand, purchase, and display the various kinds of play materials recommended for toddlers.

Warning signs	Why this might be happening	How you can help
toddlers rarely using the sand table; only a few tools available	Caregivers don't really want toddlers to play at the sand table because they think that it is too messy.	Remind caregivers of the many things toddlers learn by playing with sand. Suggest some simple props that will enhance toddlers' sand play. Discuss ways to include toddlers in the cleanup activities and ways to prevent spills. If needed, provide cleanup tools—small brooms, dustpans, or perhaps a portable vacuum cleaner—for toddlers to use.
items in the dramatic play area that seldom change	Caregivers are not conducting regular observations of children, so they don't know what props to add to extend children's dramatic play. They may think that enough items are in the dramatic play area already.	Ask caregivers to take turns observing toddlers' dramatic play and sharing their observations. Have them make a list of props to add to the dramatic play area (parents could help collect these props). Caregivers might want to add seasonal props—small snow shovels during the winter, for example—or items that relate to a recent event—extra dolls and blankets after a toddler's parent brings in the new baby to meet the class.

Program structure: Schedule and routines

Toddler classrooms follow a flexible schedule that has a somewhat predictable sequence of events and is adjusted to meet the toddlers' individual needs and to respond to special events. The schedule includes an arrival period, meal- and naptimes, indoor and outdoor play times, small-group activities, and a departure period. Small-group activities, involving three to five children, last no longer than 5 to 10 minutes. Routines (such as eating, diapering or toileting, and taking naps) make up much of the toddlers' day and are therefore used for learning. Toddlers are encouraged to actively participate in routines—for example, toileting, washing their hands, and brushing their teeth. Transitions from one activity to the next also are time consuming but important parts of the day. Toddlers participate in transitions, such as cleanup time, getting ready for mealtimes, and getting ready for outdoor play.

What you should see	Why
the daily schedule posted in the room where parents and caregivers can refer to it	A posted schedule reminds everyone of when different activities are to take place. Parents like to know what their children do at the center, and the posted schedule gives them an overview of the daily events.
the day's events occurring in the same order each day (for example, outdoor play before lunch, eating snack after naptime); a picture (photographs or drawings) version of the daily schedule posted at toddlers' eye level	Toddlers develop a sense of trust when they can predict what activity comes next. They can follow the picture schedule to learn the order of daily events; for example, their parents pick them up after free play and lunch is right before naptime. This knowledge helps them feel secure at the center.
caregivers patiently waiting for toddlers to zip their own coats, put on or take off their socks, get their blankets from their cubbies, wipe the table, and do other things for themselves	Participating in routines and transitions is an important part of a toddler's day because toddlers want and need to do things for themselves. They might take a long time to zip their coats or wipe the table, but with practice and support from adults, they learn to complete these tasks faster. When adults give them enough time to do things for themselves, toddlers know that they are learning important skills.
a caregiver leading a few toddlers in a small-group activity (for example, reading a story, fingerpainting, dancing to music, and so on)	Most toddlers are too young to participate in activities that involve the whole group. They learn more from individual attention, which can only be provided when the group is small.

What you should see	**Why**
caregivers and toddlers playing outdoors several times a day	Playing outdoors provides many opportunities for toddlers to develop and practice gross-motor skills. Being outdoors allows toddlers to release energy, get fresh air, and explore an environment that is different from the one they have indoors.
caregivers and toddlers following a regular routine to prepare for naps, and toddlers sleeping with their special blankets or toys from home	Following a predictable routine at naptime helps toddlers settle down and get needed sleep. Their special items from home help them feel secure.
a caregiver taking a small group of toddlers for an impromptu walk around the center—indoors or outdoors	Sometimes the toddler classroom can feel too crowded and overwhelming. At such times, caregivers can take a small group out of the room for a change of scenery. The toddlers will encounter many interesting things to see, hear, and touch—even the most ordinary objects and events can seem interesting to toddlers.
caregivers waiting to go outside until a child who is crying has received comfort, or staying outdoors for an extra 10 minutes because the children are still having a great time blowing bubbles and chasing them	The toddlers' schedule of daily activities must be flexible enough to meet the needs of individual children. When an activity is going well, the schedule can be adjusted so that the children can continue their enjoyment.

© April Haase

An appropriate program for toddlers (18 months to 3 years) provides a balance between a toddler's conflicting needs for security and independence. Caregivers respond to toddlers' struggles to become independent by allowing them to make simple choices and to do things for themselves.

When the program structure is not working

The following are a few warning signs that the program structure in the toddler classroom is not working. If you observe these or other warning signs, work with caregivers to analyze their schedule and their approach to involving toddlers in transitions and routines.

Warning signs	Why this might be happening	How you can help
a caregiver trying to teach a song to all of the toddlers at once	The caregivers want the toddlers to do the same kinds of activities as preschoolers do. They don't realize that toddlers cannot sit still for very long, and that large-group activities are not appropriate for this age group. Caregivers don't know how to lead an activity for only two or three toddlers.	Review with caregivers the information on appropriate toddler programs presented in *Developmentally Appropriate Practice in Early Childhood Programs Serving Children from Birth Through Age 8* (Bredekamp, 1987). Ask a caregiver to try an activity with two or three toddlers while a colleague observes and records what happens. They can use the recordings as they discuss whether the activity worked—did children enjoy and learn from the experience?
caregivers diapering toddlers as quickly as possible, without talking to the children about what they are doing	The caregivers view diapering as an unpleasant task to be rapidly dispensed with so that they can go on to other things. They don't view diapering as an opportunity to spend one-on-one time with a child.	When you visit the toddler room, offer to diaper the toddlers. While modeling this routine, talk with the toddlers and involve them in the diapering ("Lift up your legs, please"). Later, discuss with caregivers ways to let toddlers know that their bodily functions are accepted and to use routines as learning opportunities.
all toddlers who are learning to use the toilet going to the bathroom at the same time whether they need to or not, or toddlers being forced to sit on the toilet "until they go"	Caregivers want to maintain a strict, orderly schedule during the day; they think that toddlers can be forced to learn to use the toilet, or the toilet used by toddlers is not in the classroom.	Conduct a workshop on the role of adults in toilet learning. Stress the need to actively involve toddlers so that they will learn to recognize the signs that they need to use the toilet. Emphasize that adults need to encourage children's self-control, rather than forcing them to use the toilet on an adult schedule. If the toilet is down the hall, have caregivers set up a system for covering for each other when a child needs to be escorted to the bathroom.

Warning signs	Why this might be happening	How you can help
caregivers serving all the meals and feeding any toddlers who can't feed themselves without making a mess	Caregivers think that they are being conscientious when they do everything for the toddlers rather than having the children help or do things for themselves. They believe that toddlers are not able to feed themselves.	Help caregivers obtain the equipment (bibs for children who need them, small utensils, serving bowls and spoons, small cups and pitchers, sponges) needed for family-style eating. If no area of the floor is washable, caregivers can put down an old shower curtain or a piece of oilcloth. Explain that toddlers need to be independent and can do many things themselves.
toddlers waiting for the scheduled times to eat a snack, go outside, play with playdough, and so on	Caregivers believe that they are providing children with structure if they stick to the schedule for the day's activities rather than meeting children's individual needs and allowing them to make choices about what they want to do.	Talk with caregivers about why the toddler room has a schedule, emphasizing that the security toddlers feel when daily events occur in the same order will allow them to feel comfortable when the schedule changes to meet their needs and interests. Observe in the classroom and suggest ways to minimize waiting; for example, have crackers and juice on hand for hungry children who need a snack now and can't wait for the scheduled time.
departure times that are unsettling for everyone caregivers, parents, and toddlers; toddlers not ready to leave and their belongings lost or scattered around the room	Caregivers are disorganized and fail to involve the toddlers in keeping their own things together. Caregivers don't understand that reconnecting with parents at the end of the day can be stressful for toddlers.	Observe departure time in the toddler room. If needed, help caregivers reorganize and label the environment so that the toddlers will know where to put their belongings. Suggest establishing some end-of-the-day rituals to help children make the transition from the center to home.

Activities and experiences

Toddlers learn with their whole bodies and with all of their senses. The activities planned for the toddler classroom allow children to be active participants—to explore their world by pushing, rolling, filling, dumping, carrying, sliding, climbing, talking, singing, and so on. Appropriate activities for toddlers include playing active roles in routines and transitions (as discussed in the previous section), self-selected activities with a wide variety of safe toys and materials, and interactions with caregivers and other toddlers. Listed below are some examples of activities that are appropriate for toddlers.

What you should see	Why
toddlers playing at the water table with utensils such as cups, spoons, pitchers, funnels, sponges, and so on	Playing with water allows toddlers to use their senses and to explore what they can make water do. They can be successful because there are no right or wrong ways to explore water. They can socialize with other toddlers at the water table and learn about cause-and-effect while filling and emptying containers, squeezing sponges, watching the water drip through funnels, and so on.
toddlers helping prepare food (for example, mashing bananas, spreading peanut butter on crackers, or tearing lettuce)	These activities allow toddlers to use their fine-motor skills, develop good nutrition habits, learn about foods, and feel good about themselves because they are helping.
caregivers and a visiting parent sitting and talking with toddlers at lunchtime	Caregivers are showing toddlers how to participate in mealtime conversations and using this routine to help children review and plan their day, discuss important needs, and learn to associate mealtime with pleasant feelings. Parents feel more involved in their children's care if their visits to the program are welcomed and appreciated.
two or three toddlers talking and playing with small cars, trucks, or other objects at the sand table	Toddlers are developing fine-motor skills while playing with sand. They are also engaging in dramatic play by moving cars around in the sand, and they are learning social skills by talking with their friends.
caregivers talking with toddlers about what the children are doing	Toddlers' language skills are developing rapidly. By talking with the toddlers about what they are doing, caregivers help toddlers learn new words to describe their feelings and actions.

What you should see	Why
a toddler going to his cubby to get a change of clothes after wetting his pants	Accidents are an inevitable part of toilet learning. Adults can respectfully acknowledge the toddler's abilities by letting the child participate in the cleanup.
a caregiver singing and showing two toddlers how to perform a simple finger play	Simple finger plays, which are fun for toddlers to learn, promote language development, fine-motor skills, and coordination.
some toddlers playing with the same materials side by side, and some toddlers playing together	Some toddlers engage in parallel play; others are ready to begin playing together and might play house or pretend to do other familiar activities.
several toddlers crawling through a large cardboard carton; several others climbing in and out of a large laundry basket	Toddlers find numerous ways to play with these items. They develop gross-motor skills and a sense of their own size while crawling in, out, and through items or pushing things around the room.
toddlers scribbling with large crayons on paper taped to the wall	As toddlers scribble on paper, they learn what kinds of marks they can make by holding the crayon in different ways, they socialize with others who are also scribbling, and they feel the sense of control that comes from making the crayon put the marks on the paper. Large pieces of paper allow them enough room to make bold marks.
toddlers putting together puzzles, then dumping all of the pieces onto the table or floor	Toddlers are ready for puzzles with a few pieces and enjoy putting them together again and again. They also enjoy dumping things, however, and they might like dumping the puzzles as much as—or more than—they like putting them together.
toddlers helping caregivers to put the large blocks back on the shelf	Toddlers like to participate in housekeeping activities. They don't yet know that many adults consider cleaning to be a nuisance. When caregivers invite toddlers to help clean the room, the children learn that helping behaviors are valued, and they learn to take care of their environment.
a caregiver showing two toddlers how to call their parents on the toy telephone	Toddlers sometimes need an adult's help to learn how to pretend. Caregivers need to observe toddlers at play to see when modeling imaginative play would be helpful and when stepping back and allowing toddlers to use their own imaginations would be better.

When the activities are inappropriate _____

Toddlers are at a unique stage of development. They are no longer babies, but they are not yet preschoolers. They need to participate in appropriate activities that allow them to develop new skills and to practice emerging ones. Listed below are some warning signs that the activities in the toddler room are not developmentally appropriate. If you see these or other warning signs during your visits to the toddler room, work with the caregivers to plan and provide the kinds of activities that help toddlers develop independence.

Warning signs	Why this might be happening	How you can help
toddlers all doing the same art project or using materials pre-cut by the caregivers	Caregivers value the products of toddlers' efforts and think that parents want to have products made by their children to display.	Explain to caregivers that toddlers are most interested in the process of creating, not in the products. Conduct a hands-on workshop on developmentally appropriate art activities for toddlers, such as tearing paper and painting with sponges.
toddlers singing alphabet or counting songs	The caregivers are responding to the excitement that parents exhibit when their toddlers learn something related to academic subjects like reading and arithmetic.	Explain that rote songs such as these have little meaning for children. Children can repeat the sounds but don't know what they mean. Introduce the caregivers to the many children's songs that are appropriate for this age group. Encourage caregivers to make up songs about the toddlers— "Katy put on her socks today, socks today, socks today. . . ." Use role play to practice explaining to parents how the activities in the toddler room help children develop the skills they will use for the academic learning that takes place in the elementary grades.

Warning signs	Why this might be happening	How you can help
caregivers performing housekeeping tasks or talking to one another rather than playing with the toddlers	Caregivers feel self-conscious and embarrassed when they play with toddlers, or they do not understand that their active participation is an essential part of a developmentally appropriate program.	During a classroom visit, model ways to play with toddlers. Join in toddlers' imaginative play, and get down to their level by squatting, kneeling, or sitting on the floor. Provide positive feedback when caregivers play with toddlers, and let them know how their participation—nondirective—helps toddlers grow and develop.
the same activities taking place in the toddler room each day, and materials in the interest areas rarely rotated	Caregivers do not think to rotate or change the toys or materials in the environment.	Have caregivers observe the children at play to determine what materials and activities are most popular. Help caregivers put away toys and materials that children are not using. Help caregivers think of a few new items to add to each interest area. Provide resources on appropriate activities for toddlers.
caregivers making toddlers leave activities in which they are engrossed to participate in adult-directed group activities	Caregivers think that toddlers learn more from participating in activities that are planned and led by adults.	Ask caregivers to observe toddlers during free play and during an adult-led activity. Have them review their notes and list the kinds of learning that took place during each observation period. Discuss the results and help caregivers plan activities that toddlers can enter or leave as they choose, rather than ones that toddlers are forced to join.

Supportive interactions

Although caring for toddlers can be very demanding, caregivers in a developmentally appropriate program demonstrate that they appreciate the special characteristics of toddlers and convey warmth and respect to the children in their care. The caregivers have appropriate expectations for toddlers and set limits that keep the children safe while allowing them to continue to strive for independence.

What you should see	Why
caregivers warmly greeting toddlers and their parents by name when they arrive in the morning	Toddlers feel more secure at the center when caregivers welcome them and when they see their parents and the caregivers communicating with one another. A caregiver's warm, personal greeting can help parents feel comfortable about bringing their toddlers to the center.
caregivers offering toddlers choices about what to do, what toys to play with, what to eat, what book to read, and so on	Providing choices for toddlers allows them to feel a sense of control, to express their preferences, and to develop self-esteem.
caregivers helping toddlers resolve their differences by using words to express what is happening and what the toddler is feeling—"You want to play with the truck. David is playing with this truck. Let's see if there is another truck on the shelf."	Describing the problem, stating what the child seems to be feeling, and providing an alternative lets the child know that it's all right to want the truck that someone else is playing with. Children need to learn that their feelings are valued and important.

© Bm Porter/Don Franklin

Although caring for toddlers can be very demanding, caregivers in a developmentally appropriate program demonstrate that they appreciate the special characteristics of toddlers and convey warmth and respect to the children in their care. Caregivers warmly greet toddlers and their parents by name when they arrive in the morning.

What you should see	**Why**
caregivers telling children what to do, rather than what *not* to do—"You can jump on the pillows."	Toddlers are inclined to resist adult requests. When the requests are stated positively, children are more likely to comply, and they learn what they should do—not what they should *not* do.
a toddler comforting another child, who is crying	Toddlers are great mimics of adult behavior. If they have seen caregivers or other adults comforting children, toddlers are likely to copy this behavior. Watching and copying adults is one of the ways that children learn social behaviors.
a caregiver praising a toddler who has just overcome his fear of climbing to the top of the slide	Toddlers work hard at developing new skills, and they feel good about themselves when other people notice their accomplishments.
a caregiver restraining a toddler who is trying to hit another child	Sometimes telling toddlers what to do does not help them stop undesirable behavior. When toddlers hit or strike other children, caregivers may need to gently restrain the child until he or she can regain self-control. Caregivers need to step in quickly to protect the child who is at risk of getting hurt.
a caregiver helping some toddlers put on their socks and letting others put on their own socks	Caregivers need to carefully observe toddlers to know how much help to offer. If a toddler finds a task too frustrating, a caregiver should step in and help the child; if the child is ready to master the challenge, however, the caregiver should step back and allow the child to do the task alone.
caregivers comforting toddlers and letting them know that they are appreciated; for example, holding toddlers in their laps, putting their arms around children, bending down to talk to children, or using caring words	Toddlers often have trouble coping with their conflicting needs for independence and for comfort and affection. Caregivers can address these different needs by learning when to provide comfort and when to provide opportunities for children to do things for themselves.
caregivers allowing toddlers to comfort themselves for a few minutes with favorite toys or blankets	Having something special from home to keep close to them can help toddlers cope with their feelings about being separated from their families. If a toddler needs to carry his or her blanket all the time, it may be hard for the child to play. Caregivers may need to look at other ways to help the child feel secure.

When interactions are inappropriate _____

Caring for toddlers can be stressful. When you observe any of the following warning signs or other indications of problems, respond quickly and help caregivers learn appropriate ways to support toddlers as they develop self-esteem and self-discipline.

Warning signs	Why this might be happening	How you can help
a caregiver laughing at a toddler who puts her pants on backwards—"Carrie, you've got your pockets in the back. You look really silly."	The caregiver does not realize how bad a person feels when ridiculed and does not know how much damage this does to a toddler's developing sense of self.	Talk with caregivers about caring words that support toddlers as they learn new skills and overcome their fears. Provide paper and markers so that caregivers can make posters for their rooms to remind them of the kinds of words that show they care—"Would you like to hold my hand when you climb up the ladder?"
caregivers ignoring crying toddlers or telling them they are "crybabies"	Caregivers think that responding immediately to crying toddlers will spoil them or that toddlers are too old to cry.	Explain to caregivers that toddlers are still very young and that they are still developing a sense of security in the world. They cry because they have needs that are not being met. Even if a toddler's need is to express anger, this anger merits a response—"I can see that you are feeling very angry."
caregivers frequently reminding toddlers of the rules and limits in the room	There are too many rules for the toddlers to remember, or, the caregiver's expectations for toddlers' behavior are inappropriate.	Help caregivers review the limits and rules. Decide which ones are necessary and appropriate for toddlers and which can be eliminated. Suggest some positive techniques the caregivers can use to help toddlers learn to follow a few simple rules, such as giving them positive rather than negative reminders—"Keep the sand in the box."

Warning signs	Why this might be happening	How you can help
caregivers arguing with each other while the toddlers watch with frightened looks on their faces	The caregivers are having difficulty working together and don't realize that they should discuss their problems at break time or at the end of the day, when the toddlers are not present.	Meet with the caregivers to help them resolve their differences and to help them learn how to work together in the future. Explain to them that toddlers learn both positive and negative ways of behaving from watching adults, and that toddlers mimic the adult behaviors they see and hear. Also, the toddlers may believe that they have done something to cause the fight.
a caregiver screaming at a toddler from across the playground, "I told you to stop dumping the sand on the ground"	This caregiver could be feeling a high level of stress, perhaps because he or she does not have realistic expectations for toddlers' behavior and does not know how to use positive guidance techniques, or perhaps because he or she does not know how to recognize and manage stress.	Intervene as quickly as possible so that the caregiver can regain his or her composure; then, in a private meeting, explain that this kind of behavior is not acceptable because it can be damaging to children. Offer to help the caregiver learn about toddler development, positive guidance techniques, and healthy ways to manage stress. Check in with this caregiver periodically to see if he or she is developing the skills needed to support toddlers' development. In extreme cases, if the caregiver does not develop the necessary skills, you may have to suggest that the caregiver pursue a different career.

Resources for working in toddler rooms

Many of the suggested resources included in the previous chapter may also be relevant to your work in toddler rooms. The following are some additional resources you may find useful.

Carnegie Task Force on Meeting the Needs of Young Children. (1994). *Starting Points: Meeting the needs of our youngest children.* New York: Carnegie Task Force on Meeting the Needs of Young Children. (Available through NAEYC.)

Documents the "quiet crisis" affecting millions of children under age 3 and their families.

Dodge, D.T., Dombro, A.L., & Colker. L.J. (1998). *A parent's guide to infant/toddler programs.* Washington, DC: Teaching Strategies.

Shows parents how warm and responsive care—at home and in child care—helps shape the future development of infants and toddlers and their ability to learn. It outlines what and how children learn during these crucial years and suggests ways that caregivers/teachers and parents can work together. (English and Spanish editions.)

Dodge, D.T., Dombro, A.L., & Koralek, D.G. (1992). *Caring for infants and toddlers* (Vols. 1 and 2). Washington, DC: Teaching Strategies.

A comprehensive, self-instructional training program in two volumes that covers the CDA Functional Areas. A trainer's guide is also available.

Dombro, A.L., Colker, L.J., & Dodge, D.T. (1997). *The creative curriculum for infants and toddlers.* Washington, DC: Teaching Strategies.

Provides a comprehensive yet easy-to-use framework for planning and implementing a developmentally appropriate program for infants and toddlers in a center-based or family child care setting. Accompanied by a journal for caregivers/teachers implementing the curriculum.

Gonzalez-Mena, J., & Widmeyer, D.E. (1997). *Infants, toddlers, and caregivers.* Palo Alto, CA: Mayfield.

An insightful look at life in a child care setting. In addition to learning about who children are at different ages, teachers will come to appreciate that there is nothing more important than their relationship with the infants and toddlers they care for.

Greenman, J., & Stonehouse, A. (1996). *Prime times: A handbook for excellence in infant and toddler programs.* St. Paul, MN: Redleaf.

Explains the needs of infants and toddlers and of their families and caregivers and describes ways to use this information to provide quality programs.

Lally, J.R., Griffin, A., Fenichel, E., Segal, M., Szanton, E., & Weissbourd, B. (1995). *Caring for infants and toddlers in groups: Developmentally appropriate practice.* Washington, DC: Zero to Three.

Defines specialized knowledge and skills and program features that support the development of infants and toddlers.

Mack, A. (1978). *Toilet learning.* Boston: Little, Brown.

This two-part book includes background information for parents and caregivers and a picture story for children. The author presents a positive approach to toilet learning, with emphasis on the child's readiness to learn how to use the toilet with minimum adult assistance.

Miller, K. (1984). *Things to do with toddlers and twos,* and (1990) *More things to do with toddlers and twos.* Marshfield, MA: Telshare.

In these two books, Karen Miller shares her deep understanding of and affinity for toddlers, based on many years of experience as a teacher and trainer. Each book contains more than 500 tips and activities, all of which can be implemented using basic materials found in almost any classroom.

Stonehouse, A. (Ed.). (1991). *Trusting toddlers: Planning for one- to three-year-olds in child care centers.* St. Paul, MN: Toys 'n' Things Press.

Originally published by the Australian Early Childhood Association, this book features a series of chapters, each written by a different expert in the field. The authors discuss issues and problems that are unique to toddler care, discipline issues with toddlers, and staff burnout.

Van der Zande, I. (1990). *1, 2, 3 . . . The toddler years: A practical guide for parents and caregivers.* Santa Cruz, CA: Santa Cruz Toddler Care Center.

A practical guide to working with toddlers written with the staff of a toddler center.

Weitzman, E. (1992). *Learning language and loving it.* Toronto: Hanen Centre.

Based on an on-site training program for early childhood staff, this book covers language learning from birth through the preschool years. Clear and vivid examples, illustrations, and graphics make the book practical and readable.

Wilson, L.C. (1995). *Infants and toddlers, curriculum and teaching.* Albany, NY: Delmar.

This comprehensive guide to caring for infants and toddlers is an excellent resource for teachers. Part 3, "Matching Caregiver Strategies and Child Development," is a particularly useful source of information on child development and developmentally appropriate practice.

Audiovisual resources

Colker, L.J. (1995). *Observing young children: Learning to look, looking to learn.* Washington, DC: Teaching Strategies

This 30-minute videotape with user's guide trains staff and providers on how to objectively and accurately observe children. Viewers gain skills in focusing their observations in order to learn more about children, to measure children's progress, and to evaluate the effectiveness of their program.

Reed, J. (Producer), & Carter, M. (Educational consultant). (1992). *Time with toddlers*. Seattle, WA: Kidspace.

This 23-minute videotape filmed at Kidspace, an NAEYC-accredited child care center in Seattle, shows examples of respectful interactions with toddlers that foster trust and autonomy, provide for mobility and sensory exploration, model language and selective intervention, soothe separation anxiety, and create a sense of power and competency.

Further resources from NAEYC*

Buzzelli, C.A. (1992). Research in review. Young children's moral understanding: Learning about right and wrong. *Young Children, 47*(6), 47-53.

Cataldo, C.Z. (1984). Infant-toddler education. Blending the best approaches. *Young Children, 39*(2), 25-32.

Understanding how infants and toddlers differ from older children gives guidance on caregiving, needs, play and learning, environment, tasks and activities, parent/family, and administrative approaches.

Cawlfield, M.E. (1992). Velcro time: The language connection. *Young Children, 47*(4), 26-30.

Daniel, J.E. (1993). Infants to toddlers: Qualities of effective transitions. *Young Children, 48*(6), 16-21.

Edwards, L.C., & Nabors, M.L. (1993). The creative arts process: What it is and what it is not. *Young Children, 48*(3), 77-81.

Eheart, B.K., & Leavitt, R.L. (1985). Supporting toddler play. *Young Children, 40*(3), 18-22.

Francks, O.R. (1979). Scribbles? Yes, they *are* art! *Young Children, 34*(5), 15-22.

The importance of scribbling and expressive art in the life and development of young children.

Friedberg, J. (1989). Food for thought. Helping today's toddlers become tomorrow's readers: A pilot parent participation project offered through a Pittsburgh health agency. *Young Children, 44*(2), 13-16.

Fucigna, C., Ives, K.C., & Ives, W. (1982). Art for toddlers: A developmental approach. *Young Children, 37*(3), 45-51.

Toddlers' art products frequently are explorations of motor activity, their markings and paintings extensive maps of involved narratives; autonomy in their designs should be encouraged.

Furman, E. (1990). Plant a potato—Learn about life (and death). *Young Children, 46*(1), 15-20.

Furman, E. (1992). Thinking about fathers. *Young Children, 47*(4), 36-37.

Gonzalez-Mena, J. (1986). Toddlers: What to expect. *Young Children, 42*(1), 47-51.

Gottschall, S. (1989). Understanding and accepting separation feelings. *Young Children, 44*(6), 11-16.

Greenberg, P. (1991). *Character development: Encouraging self-esteem and self-discipline in infants, toddlers, and two-year-olds*. Washington, DC: NAEYC.

Hignett, W.F. (1988). Food for thought. Infant/toddler day care, yes; *but* we'd better make it good. *Young Children, 44*(1), 32-33.

Hoben, A. (1989). Caregivers' corner. Our thoughts on diapering and potty training. *Young Children, 44*(6), 28-29.

Honig, A.S. (1989). Quality infant/toddler caregiving: Are there magic recipes? *Young Children, 44*(4), 4-10.

Leavitt, R.L., & Eheart, B.K. (1991). Assessment in early childhood programs. *Young Children, 46*(5), 4-9.

Steinberg, M., Williams, S., & Da Ros, D. (1992). Caregivers' corner. Toilet learning takes time. *Young Children, 48*(1), 56.

Stewart, I.S. (1982). The real world of teaching two-year-old children. *Young Children, 37*(5), 3-13.

Understanding the developmental needs in order to prepare the physical environment; organize materials and the school day; and provide activities for physical development, cognitive learning, and social learning.

Tyler, B., & Dittmann, L. (1980). Meeting the toddler more than halfway. The behavior of toddlers and their caregivers. *Young Children, 35*(2), 39-46.

Wittmer, D.S., & Honig, A.S. (1994). Encouraging positive social development in young children. *Young Children, 49*(5), 4-12.

*To obtain a book published by NAEYC, call 800-424-2460 and ask for Resource Sales. For *Young Children* articles from the past five years, call the Institute for Scientific Information, 215-386-0100, ext. 5399, or fax 215-222-0840; from earlier issues, contact NAEYC's Public Affairs Department.

CHAPTER FOUR

Preschoolers

An appropriate preschool program provides many opportunities for children to develop their own interests and to learn to work cooperatively with others. Preschool children are at the stage of initiative—and benefit most—when they can explore and pursue activities that they select on their own. The teacher's role is one of facilitating and guiding learning, rather than providing answers or telling children how they must use materials. This section offers information and guidance to help you oversee the environment, materials and equipment, program structure, activities and experiences, and supportive interactions of teachers working with preschool children in center-based programs.

Environment

Preschool children flourish in a well-organized, clearly defined environment that is arranged to promote independence, foster decisionmaking, and encourage initiative and involvement. A well-organized preschool classroom is divided into attractive and inviting interest areas that offer children a range of activity choices. Areas set aside for dramatic play, block building, woodworking, or gross-motor activities provide opportunities for active play. Areas set aside for books, art, pets, or table toys provide opportunities for quieter play. Sometimes children want to work alone; at other times they prefer to be part of a small group. When the environment is structured so that children can work successfully with each other, it supports the development of social competence, which is an underlying goal of all early childhood programs.

A rich, well-organized environment can support teachers' goals for children, or it can work against them. Following are examples of what you should see in a center-based program serving preschool children and why these arrangements of the environment support teachers' goals.

Environment (cont'd) _____

What you should see

Why

noisy areas separated from quiet areas—for example, blocks and dramatic play located near each other, separated from books and table toys

Preschool children find focusing on quiet activities easier if they are not distracted by noise from neighboring centers. Separating the areas makes it possible for children to work successfully at all types of activities.

low furniture (such as shelves, tables and chairs, and dividers) and floor coverings (such as solid-colored carpeting or linoleum) used to create areas and work surfaces for small-group activities

Using low furniture to define work spaces helps children concentrate because they are not distracted by activities in other areas. At the same time, teachers can watch over the children to ensure their safety and to respond to their needs.

areas set up for different kinds of self-selected activities—dramatic play, art, blocks, table toys, books, sand and water, and gross-motor activities

An important goal of early childhood education is to help children learn to make individual choices. Teachers support this goal by ensuring that the choices are clear to the children so that they can select from a variety of activities, including quiet and active ones.

materials displayed on low shelves labeled with pictures or words so that children can reach what they need and replace items when they are finished

When materials are readily accessible, children can choose what they want to use. Labeling the place where each object belongs helps children maintain the environment and conveys the message that orderliness is valued. By sharing responsibility for their environment, children develop independence and self-esteem. The cleanup process promotes cognitive skills such as sorting and matching.

private hideaways and soft spaces (such as large pillows, rugs, rocking chairs, platforms, and couches) where children can relax and be alone or with friends

Children who spend long hours in a group program need soft, comforting places to relax and get away from the noise and activities. Being able to recoup their energy contributes to children's emotional well-being and encourages positive behavior.

materials displayed in the areas where children use them and logically organized, for example, crayons and markers with the drawing paper, pegs with the pegboards, block accessories in the block area

This tells children which materials belong together, suggests how materials can be used, and supports more complex play. Logical grouping of materials promotes their appropriate use.

pictures (children's work and other pictures relevant to the children's interests) hung on the walls at the children's eye level

Children do not notice pictures that are placed far above their eye level. Displaying children's work conveys respect for their efforts and gives them pride in their accomplishments.

What you should see	**Why**
an area with large-motor equipment (such as a climber or a balance beam) that can be set up within the room	Preschool children benefit from daily opportunities to exercise their large muscles. Physical development contributes to positive self-esteem as children develop confidence in their gross-motor skills.
a safe, well-organized outdoor play area including a variety of surfaces, equipment and materials for large-muscle play, and space for activities, such as painting, woodworking, and playing with water	The outdoor environment provides a new setting for children to explore and a place for them to release pent-up energy. Activities that take place indoors can be enjoyed by children in different ways when conducted outdoors.
space and materials modifed for children with disabilities	When children with disabilities are included in the regular preschool program, all children benefit.
a parent bulletin board or message center that is regularly updated with attractive displays, interesting articles, and announcements of events at the center and in the community	A place for parents conveys the message that parents are important and the staff want to keep them informed.

© Cheryl Namkung

An appropriate preschool program provides many opportunities for children to develop their own interests and to learn to work cooperatively with others. When children with disabilities are included in the regular preschool program, all children benefit.

When the environment is not working

The children's behavior can help you assess the appropriateness of the physical environment. If you regularly observe certain troublesome behaviors, consider whether the environment is contributing to the problems; for example, you might notice that children tend to

- run in the room;
- wander around looking for things to do;
- perform the same activities again and again;
- find sticking with an activity difficult;
- have extreme difficulty sharing;

- use materials destructively;
- shout from one area to the next, creating a high noise level;
- crawl under tables or on shelves;
- resist requests that they help clean up; or
- consistently depend on adults for the things they need.

Although these behaviors may result from a variety of causes, the physical environment may sometimes be at fault. In working with teachers to improve the environment, ask yourself *why* the teachers might have organized the room inappropriately. Listed below are warning signs that the environment is inappropriate for preschool children, possible reasons teachers might have for organizing the environment in these ways, and strategies you might try to improve the quality of the environment.

© Elisabeth Nichols

In a successful preschool classroom, most children are usually busy. If you regularly observe certain troublesome behaviors, help teachers consider whether or not the environment is contributing to the problems.

Warning signs	Why this might be happening	How you can help
teachers continually complaining about children's behavior	The teachers are unaware that the way they have arranged the environment may be encouraging negative behavior.	Show slides of different room arrangements and point out how the environment can affect children's behavior. Observe in the classrooms to assess whether the room arrangement is a factor in children's inappropriate behavior. Discuss your observations with teachers and help them rearrange their rooms.
shelves and furniture arranged against the wall, with lots of open spaces that encourage children to run	Teachers sometimes arrange a small room in this way to give the children more space or to ensure that they can see all of the children at once.	Help teachers arrange the space into defined areas so that they can still see the children at all times. During a classroom visit, document children's behavior and share your observations with the staff.
walls cluttered with pictures hung far above the children's eye level	Teachers may be using their own height to determine where to put displays. They want to make the room attractive.	Have teachers examine the room from a child's viewpoint, then discuss changes that could make the displays more appropriate for children.
walls and bulletin boards covered with artwork precut by adults or with decorations such as cartoon characters	Teachers may believe that having attractive displays is most important. They do not appreciate the value of displaying children's own artwork.	Explain how displaying children's work enhances their self-esteem and conveys the message that this is their classroom. Assist the teachers in attractively displaying children's work.
no soft areas where children can get away and be by themselves	Teachers may feel constrained by what furniture is provided.	Lead a discussion in which teachers describe their favorite places. Note how we all like soft, comfortable areas. Suggest inexpensive ways to make the classroom environment soft and inviting.

Equipment and materials

The success of each interest area in a preschool classroom and outdoors depends on the selection and display of the equipment and materials. Well-organized interest areas contain a rich supply of materials that are rotated and replaced often enough to maintain children's interest and continually challenge them. The materials and equipment should be appropriate for the ages and stages of the children in the group and should match and challenge the children's skills and knowledge. Children need to experience success and at the same time to be sufficiently challenged to learn new skills and concepts.

If, during your classroom visits, you notice that the materials are not developmentally appropriate or that the displays are poorly organized, you may need to work with the teachers to improve the equipment and materials. Listed below are suggestions for what to include in each interest area of a preschool classroom.*

Block corner

- carpet (nonpatterned) or tape to define the block area
- a complete set of hardwood unit blocks (approximately 400 pieces for 15 to 18 children)
- hollow blocks
- decorative items
  - set of colored cube blocks
  - Legos (large)
- people props
  - multiethnic sets of families
  - a wooden set of multiethnic community helpers
- animal props
  - farm and/or zoo animals
- transportation props
  - large and small cars, trucks, fire engines, trains, buses, and airplanes (at least two of each)
  - traffic signs
- dollhouse furniture
  - beds, chairs, and tables (at least two of each)

House corner

- table and four chairs
- highchair
- doll bed
- stove
- refrigerator
- sink
- baby dolls that are representative of several ethnic backgrounds, including those of the children in the program
- doll clothes and blankets
- pots, pans, and utensils
- broom and/or mop
- safety mirror—full length
- dishes (one set)
- telephones (at least two)
- male and female dressup clothes
- hats
- costume jewelry
- purses, tote bags, and/or suitcases
- prop boxes for themes, such as barber shop and grocery store

*From Dodge, D.T. (1993). *A guide for supervisors and trainers on implementing the creative curriculum for early childhood* (3rd ed.). Washington, DC: Teaching Strategies, Inc.

Table toy area

- puzzles (wooden, rubber inserts, and cardboard)
- sewing cards and yarn
- Legos
- lotto games
- beads for stringing
- pegs and pegboards (at least two)
- colored inch-cube blocks
- parquetry or pattern blocks
- interlocking toys
- stacking rings or nesting cubes (two sets)
- simple games, such as memory and color-matching games
- attribute blocks
- objects to sniff, smell, and taste, such as cinnamon, onions, coffee, lemons, orange peels, nutmeg, and cloves
- objects to feel, sort, and classify, such as shells, stones, pebbles, seeds, nuts, and leaves
- collectibles, such as buttons, bottle caps, and keys
- Cuisenaire™ rods
- table blocks (hardwood)
- self-help frames for learning skills, such as buttoning, zipping, and tying
- dramatic play props, such as doll furniture, a small family set, and animals

Art area

- old tablecloth or plastic for floor covering
- painting supplies
  - easel
  - paints
  - paint containers
  - paintbrushes
  - newsprint
- drying rack for paintings
- felt-tip markers (nontoxic and washable)
- glue and/or paste

- white and colored chalk
- large crayons
- drawing paper
- safety scissors for left- and right-handed children
- fingerpaints (homemade or purchased) and paper
- trays for fingerpainting
- clay and homemade playdough
- assorted-color construction paper
- smocks (donated old shirts or plastic smocks)
- materials for collages
- yarn
- tagboard, cardboard, or Styrofoam™ trays
- hole punch
- stapler and staples

Library

- carpeted floor
- rocking chair, soft chair, mattress, and pillows
- bookstand, in which the displayed book covers face the viewer
- commercial and homemade books about
  - feelings and attitudes
  - families and friends
  - everyday experiences
  - science and nature
  - fun and fantasy
- sets of books and cassette tapes and a tape player
- puppets
- typewriter or personal computer
- writing tools, such as pencils, crayons, chalk, and felt-tip markers
- printing tools, such as stamps and ink pads
- paper, such as computer-printout paper and index cards
- tools, such as scissors, hole punch, and stapler

Equipment and materials (cont'd)

Sand and water play area

- table or basins for sand or water
- plastic props, such as measuring cups, funnels, shovels, spoons, squirt bottles, and basting tools
- plastic smocks for water play
- buckets, sponges, brooms, and mops for cleanup

Motor development and music area

- CD player and CDs or tape recorder and cassettes
- instruments for adults, such as a piano, an autoharp, and a guitar
- homemade and commercial rhythm instruments, such as drums and triangles
- scarves and streamers
- small parachute

Woodworking area

- woodworking bench or tree stump that has been treated with nontoxic preservative

- real, child-size tools, such as hammer, saws, vise, chisel, screwdrivers, hand drill, and pliers
- nails, screws, ruler, carpenters' pencils, and corks
- scraps and boards of hard and soft wood

Outdoor area

- swings, slides, and climbers
- tricycles, wheelbarrows, and wagons
- balls (several sizes)
- jump ropes
- sandbox area with sand, shovels, buckets, spoons, bowls, gelatin molds, plastic bottles (cut in half), funnels, and so on
- water table or a plastic basin, pails and buckets, and large house-painting brushes for water play
- large boxes
- tires, boards, and sawhorses
- garden tools, rakes, and shovels

© Esther Mugar

In many preschools, much-used areas for sand and water play, motor development and music, woodworking, and outdoor play are lacking. Help teachers understand why these activities are important and how to create an environment that encourages them.

When visiting preschool classrooms, you have an opportunity to assess the equipment and materials the teachers have selected and displayed for children. Even classrooms that are not fully equipped can successfully address the needs of preschool children if they meet the following criteria.

What you should see	Why
materials (such as dolls from different ethnic groups and picture books showing people of many cultures) relevant to the cultural backgrounds and life experiences of the children	Children respond to materials that are relevant to their own experiences. Providing culturally relevant materials enhances children's self-esteem by making them feel accepted and respected.
materials and equipment in good repair, with no sharp edges, peeling paint, splinters, or other hazards	To ensure children's safety, teachers regularly check all materials and equipment, removing unsafe items or making sure that they are repaired.
a sufficient quantity of basic materials, such as table toys and blocks, and multiple sets of popular items	Before young children are able to share, they need a period of time when the demands to share are minimal.
materials in each interest area that reflect the curriculum and the specific interests of the children; for example, if children have been regularly visiting a nearby construction site, you might see hard hats and lunch pails in the dramatic play area; large toggle hooks, pipes, and construction vehicles in the block area; and books on buildings in the book area	Children learn by interacting with materials and re-creating their experiences. They are more likely to do this when the materials in each interest area reflect their experiences and interests.
materials that vary in complexity; for example, 5-piece puzzles as well as 10- and 12-piece puzzles; playdough and a box of utensils	Children of similar ages vary widely in stages of development. Materials and equipment should be appropriate for varied skill levels, enabling all children to experience success.
nonsexist materials evident in all interest areas, such as men's and women's dressup clothes, community-helper props showing men and women in all roles, and books and pictures showing women in leadership roles and men in nurturing roles	Children will learn that boys and girls can assume nurturing roles in the family as well as a wide range of jobs and professions.
soft materials (such as playdough, fingerpaints, clay, sand, and water) offered daily as an activity option	Soft materials help children relax and soothe away the stress that can come from being in a group setting all day.
toys with small pieces stored in dishpans or other clearly labeled containers	Appropriate storage containers allow children to find what they need without having to spill everything.

PRESCHOOLERS

75

When equipment and materials are inappropriate

A number of warning signs can alert you to the fact that teachers need help with selecting and displaying materials and equipment. Considering the possible causes for these problems helps you identify appropriate strategies.

Warning signs	Why this might be happening	How you can help
toys not attractively displayed or organized; materials used together not displayed together; some toys missing pieces	Teachers may believe that, because children use all of the toys every day, taking the time to put them away in an organized manner is a waste of time.	Explain what children learn when they play in a well-organized environment and how adults and children are likely to feel when they work in disorganized spaces. Demonstrate how cleanup teaches children self-discipline, enhances their self-esteem, and helps them learn cognitive skills, such as matching and sorting.
the same materials out day after day, and the children seeming bored with them	Teachers may not think they have options or may believe that they lack the resources to get new materials.	Conduct a workshop to organize materials and make new ones for the classroom. Set up a system for sharing materials. Involve teachers in selecting new materials for the center.

© Francis Wardle

Explain what children learn when they play in a well-organized environment and how adults and children are likely to feel when they work in disorganized spaces. Conduct a workshop to organize materials and make new ones for the classroom.

Warning signs	Why this might be happening	How you can help
children depending on adults and appearing frustrated when they can't get immediate assistance	The materials selected by the teachers may be too difficult for the children to handle on their own.	Review the list of basic equipment and materials with the teachers. Help teachers assess the children's skills and determine which materials are appropriate and which should be replaced.
children failing to return materials when they are finished using them; at cleanup time, materials placed anywhere in the room or mixed together	The teachers have not established a place for everything in the classroom or put labels on shelves and containers.	Plan a workshop to make labels for the materials in the classroom. Reinforce the value of labeling materials.
boys ignoring the dramatic play area, and girls rarely selecting the block corner or gross-motor area	The equipment and materials in these areas may convey messages that make some children feel that they are not welcome there.	Meet with the teachers to discuss what messages the equipment and materials convey to girls and boys and talk about ways to encourage nonsexist play. Help teachers examine their own attitudes about the roles of men and women in our society.
children using materials in a repetitive way, then losing interest quickly and moving on to another activity	The same materials have been out every day, and the children are bored with them. The materials are too simple and fail to challenge the children.	Discuss ways to make basic materials more challenging; for example, add new utensils for playdough or new props in the block area. Help teachers observe children during self-selected activities and note what equipment and materials they select and how they use them.
children continually fighting over materials and toys	Teachers provide an insufficient number of choices that interest the children, and the demands for sharing are too great.	Help the teachers to note which materials are most popular and provide duplicates of popular materials. Offer materials that will be of interest to the children.

Program structure: Schedule and routines

The program structure provides the framework for the day's events. When followed consistently, this structure gives children a sense of security. The time allocated for each period should reflect a recognition of preschool children's needs, interests, and abilities; for example, active and quiet periods should be balanced during the day. Because preschool children can become quite involved in an activity, large chunks of time (an hour or more) are appropriate for self-selected activities and outdoor activities, weather permitting. Periods when preschool children are in a large group (such as circle or storytime) should be short—no more than 10 or 15 minutes. An appropriate program structure reflects the developmental abilities of the children.

Sample Schedule for a Preschool Program

7:30 – 8:30	Arrival and quiet activities
8:30 – 9:00	Breakfast and cleanup
9:00 – 9:15	Meeting
9:15 – 10:30	Self-selected activities
10:30 – 10:45	Cleanup
10:45 – 11:30	Outdoor self-selected activities
11:30 – Noon	Storytime and preparations for lunch
Noon – 12:45	Lunch, cleanup, and preparations for naps
12:45 – 2:30	Naps and quiet activities
2:30 – 3:00	Snack and preparations to go outdoors
3:00 – 4:00	Outdoor time
4:00 – 5:00	Self-selected activities
5:00 – 6:00	Cleanup, preparations to go home, quiet activities, departures

Transitions are the in-between times when children are moving from one activity to the next—from cleanup to circle time, from outdoor play to lunch preparation and lunchtime. Transitions can become problem periods if children don't know what is expected. Waiting is difficult for young children, and unless they are purposefully occupied, they might find something to do that does not fit in with the teachers' plans.

Similarly, making routines (such as eating meals and taking naps) comfortable for children and using the routines as learning times can greatly enhance the daily program and make life easier for teachers. Following are examples of an appropriate program structure and how it supports preschool children's growth and development.

What you should see	**Why**
a balance of active and quiet times; for example, outdoor time and music activities alternating with storytime and rest periods	Young children need lots of active play, but they also tire easily. An appropriate schedule provides for both expending and recouping energy.
children spending at least two periods outdoors every day	Children need fresh air and a place to run and jump and play. Learning can just as effectively take place in the outdoor environment.
time periods appropriate for the children's developmental abilities	Behavior problems can be minimized by adjusting the schedule to the children's developmental abilities. Preschool children cannot be expected to sit still for 30 to 45 minutes of circle time—15 minutes would be more appropriate.
sufficient time allocated for children to select their own activities and to play for an extended time; for example, at least one hour of self-selected activities in the morning and one hour in the afternoon	Children learn best when they can select activities that interest them and when they have time to see projects through to completion. Increasingly complex thinking skills develop when children have the time to fully explore an experience.
teachers giving children sufficient warning to complete what they are doing and prepare for the next activity; for example, "In five minutes it will be time for . . ."	Preschool children can become very involved in activities and find stopping what they are doing difficult. They are more likely to cooperate when they are given a warning and have time to complete what they have started.
children meaningfully involved during transition activities, such as washing paintbrushes, setting tables for a meal, or preparing the cots for naps; teachers talking to children during routines, such as during meals and when preparing for rest	Routines provide excellent opportunities for children to learn new concepts and skills and for teachers to engage children in conversations to get to know them better. Helping to maintain the environment makes children feel competent and responsible.
a relaxed atmosphere at meals; eating with children and engaging them in conversations; not rushing children or forcing them to finish everything	Children digest their food better in a calm atmosphere in which they are encouraged to try new foods but are not required to finish everything. They can learn about different foods and acquire social skills during meals.
teachers and children serving themselves family-style (from bowls passed around the table)	When children are allowed to serve themselves, they learn to make judgments about how much they can eat and they develop fine-motor control.

When the program structure is not working

Observing in the classroom enables you to assess whether the program structure is working well for preschool children. If you note any of the warning signs listed below, review the possible causes before designing approaches to help the teachers resolve the problems.

Warning signs	Why this might be happening	How you can help
children appearing confused about where they are expected to be and what they are expected to be doing	The teachers do not follow a consistent schedule, so the children must depend on adults to direct them.	Share the sample schedule with teachers and help them develop one for their room. Suggest illustrating the schedule with pictures to help children learn the daily sequence of events.
children sitting for long periods of time—for example, during circle time	Teachers may believe that circle time is the best time to teach children new skills and concepts, that "teaching is telling," and that children learn by listening.	Refer teachers to *Developmentally Appropriate Practice in Early Childhood Programs Serving Children From Birth Through Age 8* (Bredekamp, 1987) and discuss how preschool children learn best through active play. Suggest adjustments to the schedule.
children going outside only in good weather; on cold days, the outdoor play period limited to 10 minutes	Teachers may not dress adequately for outdoors. Parents don't want their children to go outside when the weather is cold or windy.	Explain the importance of daily fresh air and gross-motor activities and suggest a minimum period for outdoor play. Discuss ways to make sure that parents understand the importance of outdoor play and the need to dress their children appropriately. Suggest that teachers keep extra mittens, hats, and sweaters for themselves and for children who do not bring appropriate clothing.

Warning signs	Why this might be happening	How you can help
teachers scolding children for not staying in line and being orderly during daily routines; children wandering away from the group	Teachers do not plan for transitions. They try to maintain order by having the whole group go through routines at the same time.	Generate a list of strategies teachers can use to make transitions run more smoothly, and post the list in the room as a reminder. Point out how much easier transitions can be when children are occupied.
teachers using activity time as a break time, organizing choices for the children but not actively interacting with the children or extending their play	Teachers sometimes fail to appreciate how much learning takes place during self-selected activity time. They do not know how to facilitate children's learning during play.	Show a videotape of children at play, and have teachers focus their attention on what children are learning in each area and how teachers are involved. Use their observations to discuss the role of adults during self-selected activities.
teachers assuming most of the routine tasks, such as preparing tables for meals, setting out cots, and cleaning up while children wait for the next activity	Teachers do not see routines as learning opportunities. They believe that completing tasks themselves is most efficient.	In a workshop have teachers brainstorm what children can learn doing different routines. Help teachers plan ways to involve the children in the routines and to promote their independence.
teachers supervising mealtimes, serving each child, and expecting children to eat everything on their plates	Mealtimes are not considered an important part of the program or recognized as opportunities for learning. Perhaps teachers value neatness more than independence and impose adult standards on the children.	Share resources on family-style eating, and discuss the importance of using mealtimes as social and learning times. Provide a list of specific strategies that teachers can try to enhance mealtimes.
children running aimlessly during outdoor time, which is unplanned and unstructured	Teachers view outdoors as recess and fail to organize the outdoor environment or plan specific activities.	Ask teachers what they see as the problems with the outdoor period. In responding to the problems, offer suggestions for making the outdoor period a time for meaningful learning activities.

Activities and experiences

Preschool children are active learners who are curious about how and why things work. When their explorations are encouraged, they develop confidence in their ability to learn. Preschool children are increasingly social and need many opportunities to relate positively to their peers and to develop friendships. Appropriate activities and experiences for preschool children include opportunities to engage in dramatic play, construct with blocks and art materials, explore natural materials like sand and water, and solve problems using manipulative toys. Listed below are examples of what you should see during an observation and explanations of how these kinds of activities and experiences enhance children's growth and development.

What you should see	Why
children working in small groups on cooperative activities, such as building with blocks, carrying equipment outdoors, or re-creating a restaurant in the dramatic play area	Most preschool children are ready to engage in cooperative play. They can discuss what they will play, assign roles, and work toward a common goal.
children working independently on tasks or activities that they have chosen for themselves, such as putting together a puzzle, painting a picture, or washing the tables	Preschool children can be very self-directed. They feel competent when they can complete tasks independently.
children purposefully building with blocks, measuring sand and water, sorting and classifying materials, drawing and painting, and observing changes around them	Learning is more meaningful to children when they can try out their ideas and see the results of their actions.
children selecting from a variety of activities that use and develop their gross-motor skills, such as playing with balls, jumping rope, climbing on equipment, and riding tricycles	The development of physical coordination and the acquisition of motor skills promotes children's self-esteem.
children engaging in activities that use and develop their fine-motor skills, such as placing pegs in a board, rolling playdough, fingerpainting, and constructing with small blocks	These activities help children develop and practice their fine-motor skills, which they will use later to write and perform other refined tasks.
children demonstrating creativity, using their imagination, and expressing themselves freely by making collages, telling stories, and participating in dramatic play	By expressing their ideas, children learn to think abstractly, which prepares them for learning to read. To read, children must understand that words represent ideas.

What you should see

children showing an interest in language and literacy activities by looking at books, drawing pictures, writing signs and stories, dictating stories, and expressing their ideas

children working together on projects, such as making a mural, planning an event, re-creating a city in the block corner, or preparing a meal

teachers involving small groups of children in cooperative tasks, such as making playdough, planting seeds, or playing a classification game

teachers regularly observing children during daily activities and documenting what they have learned about each child's abilities and interests

teachers asking open-ended questions designed to encourage children to think and express their ideas; teachers accepting more than one answer as correct and encouraging individual thinking.

children engaging in activities that involve mathematical thinking, such as measuring ingredients for a baking project, comparing lengths of Cuisenaire rods, and making graphs

family members participating in the daily program by sharing their skills and interests and working with the children

Why

These early explorations of reading and writing are evidence of emerging literacy.

Working together helps children learn to respect the ideas of others, to contribute to joint efforts, to solve problems, and to develop social skills.

Activities initiated by children should be balanced with activities initiated by teachers. What is always important is that children are actively involved.

Teachers facilitate children's growth and learning by observing children each day and using the insights they gain to plan activities, adapt the environment, and intervene to extend children's learning.

An important goal during the preschool years is to help children develop self-confidence as learners and to promote creative thinking. When teachers respect children's responses, children are more likely to share their ideas.

Preschool children develop mathematical thinking skills by playing with toys and objects that they can classify, compare, measure, and order. They may already know how to count by rote, but they need many opportunities to play and work with materials to understand that numerals are symbols for numbers.

When children see that members of their family are connected to the life at the center, they feel that their two worlds are connected. Participating in the curriculum enables parents to better understand its philosophy and goals and to enrich the program itself.

When the activities are inappropriate

Observing in preschool classrooms, you might not see children and teachers engaged in activities like the ones previously described. The following warning signs should make you question whether the activities planned and implemented are developmentally appropriate.

Warning signs	Why this might be happening	How you can help
teachers directing activities for the whole group at one time, expecting children to sit quietly and follow directions	This way of structuring activities may be similar to what the teachers themselves experienced in school, and they believe that this is an appropriate role of teachers.	Help teachers to focus on the environment as the setting for appropriate activities and to design ways of enriching the environment to support learning. Work with teachers to design activities and experiences that children can self-select and that can be enjoyed by children playing individually or in small groups.
teachers cutting shapes for the children to use in prescribed ways and emphasizing product-oriented art projects	Teachers value the product more than the process of art because they want the children to have something to show their parents and to display in the classroom.	Conduct a workshop in which the teachers color a detailed drawing with their non-dominant hand. Then offer a creative and unstructured art activity. Have teachers compare the two experiences and discuss how creative art activities promote children's growth and development.
children filling out ditto sheets and workbooks that the teachers correct	Because these activities keep children quiet, teachers mistakenly believe that children learn from them. Teachers may use these activities to fill in the schedule because they have not planned appropriately.	Clarify why ditto sheets are inappropriate and should not be used in a child development program: they stifle children's creative expression and do not promote meaningful learning.
activities that stress academic learning through activities such as recognizing and writing the alphabet and numbers, coloring pre-drawn shapes, and memorizing facts	Teachers believe that they have to "teach" children so they will be ready for school.	Share resources that describe the research on pushing children into abstract learning too early. Provide specific ideas of activities they can plan and implement to help children develop the skills they need for reading, writing, and mathematical thinking.

Warning signs	**Why this might be happening**	**How you can help**
teachers admonishing children to sit still, listen quietly, raise their hands if they have something to say, and take turns answering questions posed by the teachers	Again, teachers may believe that these are appropriate behaviors for children who will soon be going to elementary school.	Suggest other ways to handle group time—for example, breaking into smaller groups or planning active games. Model an appropriate large-group activity for the teachers.

© Robert J. Bennett

There are so many wonderful learning activities! Work with teachers to design activities and experiences that children can self-select and that can be enjoyed by children playing individually or in small groups.

Supportive interactions

The atmosphere in a preschool classroom reflects the quality of the interactions. Lively chatter can be heard from children talking and working together and from teachers reacting to children's ideas, questions, and concerns. Teachers are genuinely interested in what the children are doing, how they are feeling, and what they have to say. The teachers' expectations for each child are appropriate to what that child can understand and do at his or her stage of development. An atmosphere of cooperation and caring is evident.

What you should see	Why
teachers responding quickly and positively to children's needs and questions, comforting distressed children, and helping them deal with their problems constructively	Children develop a sense of trust and self-esteem when adults are responsive to their needs. They learn that they are important and worthy people.
teachers bending, kneeling, or sitting down to establish eye contact when talking to children	Eye contact promotes good communication. Children feel more respected when adults are at their level.
teachers giving attention to children who are less verbal, as well as to those who have a lot to say and who demand their attention	Children who are quiet are sometimes forgotten, but they also need adults' attention. When teachers make a point to get to know each child, they are more likely to address each child's needs.
teachers showing respect for children's feelings and ideas, even if they disagree with them	When the teachers acknowledge and show respect for children's feelings, children learn that they are valued and their self-esteem is enhanced.
teachers reminding children of the classroom rules and applying them consistently and calmly	Children are more likely to follow the rules when they know what is expected of them and when they believe the rules and limits are enforced fairly.
teachers describing the behavior they want to see in positive terms—"Keep the water inside the water table. The floor gets slippery if it's wet."	When teachers give children a clear statement of what they can do as well as what behavior is not acceptable, children learn what is expected of them and are more likely to change their behavior accordingly.
children discussing and resolving their conflicts on their own or with the teacher's support when necessary	Teachers can help children develop social skills, such as cooperation, negotiation, and problem solving, by teaching them to express their feelings in words and to resolve conflicts peacefully.

What you should see	Why
teachers planning activities that involve children in cooperative efforts and encouraging children to work together, help each other, and care for one another	Social competence is an underlying goal of early childhood education. Children who learn to work with others and develop friendships are more likely to succeed in school and in life.
children willing to listen to other points of view and to accept individual differences	The ability to see things from another perspective is an important cognitive skill and is critical to living successfully in a group.
teachers providing encouragement and suggestions to enable children to solve problems on their own, complete challenging tasks, and learn from their mistakes	Encouragement and support promote children's confidence, self-esteem, and understanding of new concepts. Children who feel good about themselves are more likely to attempt challenges that will help them develop new skills.
teachers helping children make friends and supporting each child's efforts to renegotiate friendships as necessary	The ability to make friends and renegotiate friendships is central to children's mental health. Children who leave the preschool years feeling friendless are likely to experience social and learning problems in later life.
parents being greeted by name when they enter the room and teachers taking time to talk with them about their child's day	Personal greetings are affirming and help to build a relationship of trust. Informal daily communications are one of the best ways to keep parents informed of their child's life at school.

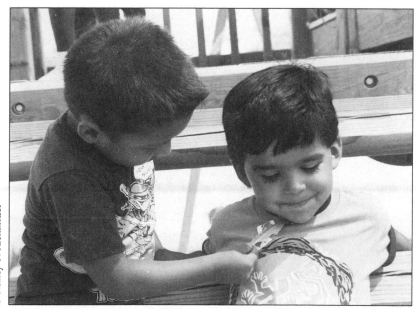

© Nancy P. Alexander

Social competence is an underlying goal of early childhood education. Children who learn to work with others and develop friendships are more likely to succeed in school and in life.

When interactions are inappropriate

You can feel the difference when you walk into a classroom where the social interactions are not appropriate. If you see the following warning signs or other similar indications of problems, work with the teachers to make the climate more supportive for the children.

Warning signs	Why this might be happening	How you can help
Children sitting in a "time-out" chair if they break rules or seem out of control	Teachers see this as an acceptable alternative to physical punishment and have few other strategies to employ in guiding children's behavior.	Clarify any misunderstandings that the teachers might have about appropriate disciplinary policies. Suggest alternative ways of guiding behavior, including talking with children, using logical consequences, and involving children in establishing rules of the classroom.
teachers focusing on children's misbehavior and failing to deal with the problems that are causing it	The misbehaving child who demands attention is easier to notice.	Conduct several observations of a child whose behavior is troublesome. Discuss what you learned and help teachers to see the value of looking at the causes behind children's misbehavior.
teachers talking down to children or shouting from across the room	Teachers do not appreciate the importance of making eye contact with children and believe that loud voices are more effective.	Discuss how a child feels and typically reacts when an adult shouts at them. Ask teachers to make a commitment to use normal voice levels and kneel down to children's eye level when speaking with the children.
teachers frequently correcting children and belittling them for forgetting the rules	Teachers do not have the skills or knowledge to guide children's behavior in positive ways.	Develop a handout that shows how to set clear limits and communicate these limits to preschoolers. Share information on indicators of child abuse, particularly emotional abuse, and be alert to evidence of abuse in the center.

Warning signs	Why this might be happening	How you can help
teachers setting standards for behavior that are not appropriate for children—for example, making children share or wait too long between activities	Teachers lack knowledge of normal child development and believe that their role is to help children conform to adult standards.	Discuss realistic expectations and how the teachers could modify their expectations in light of what they have learned about child development.
parents dropping their children off and leaving quickly without talking to teachers or observing the program	Teachers have conveyed the message to parents that children fare better if the transition is brief.	Explain how important it is for children to see that their parents and teachers have established a positive relationship.

© Nancy P. Alexander

Children develop a sense of trust and self-esteem when adults are responsive to their needs. They learn that they are important and worthy people. Children who are quiet are sometimes forgotten, but they also need adults' attention. When teachers make a point to get to know each child, they are more likely to address each child's needs.

Resources for working in preschool classrooms ————

Bos, B. (1984). *Please don't move the muffin tins: A hands-off guide to art for the young child.* Roseville, CA: Turn-the-Page Press.

A collection of developmentally appropriate art experiences for young children.

Cherry, C. (1985). *Parents, please don't sit on the kids.* Belmont, CA: David S. Lake.

Contains many practical suggestions for guiding children's behavior, explaining techniques that work with young children and those that don't.

Dodge, D.T., & Colker, L.J. (1992). *The creative curriculum for early childhood* (3d ed.). Washington, DC: Teaching Strategies.

A comprehensive curriculum appropriate for children from 3 to 5 years old; offers practical strategies based on child development theory for setting the stage and promoting learning in 10 interest areas: blocks, house corner, table toys, art, sand and water, library, music and movement, cooking, computers, and outdoors.

Dodge, D.T., Koralek, D.G., & Pizzolongo, P.J. (1996). *Caring for preschool children* (Vols. 1 and 2, 2d ed.) Washington, DC: Teaching Strategies.

A comprehensive, self-instructional training program in two volumes that covers the 13 CDA functional areas. Also available is a trainer's guide that explains how to oversee the training program and help teachers assess their progress.

Edwards, C., Gandini, L., & Forman, G. (Eds.) (1993). *The hundred languages of children: The Reggio Emilia approach to early childhood education.* Norwood, NJ: Ablex.

Describes the philosophy, methods, environments, and possible applications of the early childhood teaching approaches implemented in the early childhood programs of Reggio Emilia, Italy.

Greenman, J. (1988). *Caring spaces, learning places: Children's environments that work.* Redmond, WA: Exchange Press.

Shows how to create environments that make use of space creatively and with attention to children's developmental needs. Richly illustrated with photographs that show children using indoor and outdoor space.

Hirsch, E.S. (Ed.). (1996). *The block book* (3d ed.). Washington, DC: NAEYC.

An illustrated book that describes how and what children can learn using blocks, including math concepts, science, social studies, self-awareness, and more.

Jalongo, M.R. (1988). *Young children and picture books: Literature from infancy to six.* Washington, DC: NAEYC.

An excellent book for caregivers on what constitutes high-quality literature and art for young children and how children benefit from good books.

Katz, L.G., & McClellan, D.E. (1997). *Fostering children's social competence: The teacher's role.* Washington, DC: NAEYC.

Suggests principles and strategies to guide teachers in strengthening children's social skills and identifies well-intentioned practices very common in early childhood classrooms that actually undermine children's social competence.

Katz, L.G., & Chard. S. (1989). *Engaging children's minds: The project approach.* Norwood, NJ: Ablex.

Provides an overview of the project approach, a strategy that supports children as they explore a topic of interest over an extended period of time. Readers learn how to respond to children's interests and skills throughout all stages of the project.

Levin, D. (1997). *Remote control childhood? Combating the hazards of media culture.* Washington, DC: NAEYC.

Provides effective guidance and strategies to minimize harmful media effects and to reshape the media environment in which children grow up.

Miller, K. (1989). *The outside play and learning book.* Mt. Rainier, MD: Gryphon House.

A comprehensive, creative collection of outdoor activities that includes many suggestions for making good use of the outdoor environment in all seasons.

Raines, S.C., & Canady, R.J. (1989). *Story s-t-r-e-t-c-h-e-r-s: Activities to expand children's favorite books*, and (1991) *More story s-t-r-e-t-c-h-e-r-s.* Mt. Rainier, MD: Gryphon House.

Filled with activities that caregivers and parents can use to extend children's enjoyment of their favorite books. Five active learning experiences are described for each of the 90 books included.

Schickedanz, J.A. (1998). *More than the ABCs: The early stages of reading and writing* (rev. ed.). Washington, DC: NAEYC.

A practical book filled with ideas for organizing the environment so that children experience reading and writing as a meaningful part of their lives.

Slaby, R.G., Roedell, W.C., Arezzo, D., & Hendrix, K. (1995). *Early violence prevention: Tools for teachers of young children.* Washington, DC: NAEYC.

Brings early childhood educators the latest knowledge on effective teaching strategies for early violence prevention. Includes chapters on helping children with aggressive behavior patterns, encouraging voluntary sharing, and teaching assertiveness skills.

Weitzman, E. (1992). *Learning language and loving it.* Toronto: Hanen Centre.

Based on an on-site training program for early childhood staff, this book covers language learning from birth through the preschool years. Clear and vivid examples, illustrations, and graphics make the book practical and readable.

Audiovisual resources

Clay, C.D. (Producer). (1998). *Read with me* and *Read with me: The teacher-parent partnership.* Washington, DC: Reading Is Fundamental.

Strategies for reading aloud with preschoolers at home and in center settings. In the first videotape, two families describe their at-home reading routines. The second depicts literacy environments in two Head Start classrooms and shows how the teachers work with families to encourage reading aloud and to build on children's interest in gaining emerging literacy skills. Video guide with handouts included.

Colker, L.J. (1995). *Observing young children: Learning to look, looking to learn.* Washington, DC: Teaching Strategies.

This 30-minute videotape with user's guide trains staff and providers on how to objectively and accurately observe children. Promotes skills in focusing observations in order to learn more about children, to measure children's progress, and to evaluate the effectiveness of their program.

Duffy, C. (Producer), & Dodge, D.T. (Director). (1988). *The creative curriculum.* Washington, DC: Teaching Strategies.

A 37-minute videotape filmed in five different preschool classrooms that shows how teachers set the stage for learning by creating a dynamic, well-organized environment. The video covers eight modules in *The Creative Curriculum* and explains how children learn in each area.

Duffy, C. (Producer), & Dodge, D.T. (Director). (1991). *The new room arrangement as a teaching strategy.* Washington, DC: Teaching Strategies.

A 15-minute slide/videotape that presents concrete ideas for arranging preschool classrooms to support positive behavior and learning.

Further resources from NAEYC*

Barbour, N., Webster, T.D., & Drosdeck, S. (1987). Sand: A resource for the language arts. *Young Children, 42*(2), 20-25.

Barclay, K.D., & Walwer, L. (1992). Linking lyrics and literacy through song picture books. *Young Children, 47*(4), 76-85.

Bender, J. (1978). Large hollow blocks. Relationship of quantity to block building behaviors. *Young Children, 33*(6), 17-23.

Betz, C. (1992). The happy medium. *Young Children, 47*(3), 34-35.

Brown, T.M., & Laminack, L.L. (1989). Let's talk a poem. *Young Children, 44*(6), 49-52.

Bundy, B.F. (1991). Fostering communication between parents and preschools. *Young Children, 46*(2), 12-17.

Buzzelli, C.A., & File, N. (1989). Building trust in friends. *Young Children, 44*(3), 70-75.

Carlsson-Paige, N., & Levin, D.E. (1992). Making peace in violent times: A construc-tivist approach to conflict resolution. *Young Children, 48*(1), 4-13.

Cartwright, S. (1987). Group endeavor in nursery school can be valuable learning. *Young Children, 42*(5), 8-11.

Cartwright, S. (1990). Learning with large blocks. *Young Children, 45*(3), 38-41.

Cartwright, S. (1993). Cooperative learning can occur in any kind of program. *Young Children, 48*(2), 12-14.

Chenfeld, M.B. (1990). "My loose is tooth!" Kidding around with the kids. *Young Children, 46*(1), 56-60.

Chenfeld, M.B. (1991). "Wanna play?" *Young Children, 46*(6), 4-6.

Christie, J.F., & Wardle, F. (1992). How much time is needed for play? *Young Children, 47*(3), 28-32.

Clemens, S.G. (1991). Art in the classroom: Making every day special. *Young Children, 46*(2), 4-11.

Clewett, A.S. (1988). Guidance and discipline: Teaching young children appropriate behavior. *Young Children, 43*(4), 26-31.

Coleman, M. (1991). Planning for the changing nature of family life in schools for young children. *Young Children, 46*(4), 15-20.

Conlon, A. (1992). Giving Mrs. Jones a hand: Making group storytime more pleasurable and meaningful for young children. *Young Children, 47*(3), 14-18.

Crosser, S. (1992). Managing the early childhood classroom. *Young Children, 47*(2), 23-29.

Delventhol, M. (1991). This is my story—This is my song. *Young Children, 46*(6), 16-18.

Written by the mother of a physically challenged child.

Dighe, J. (1993). Children and the Earth. *Young Children, 48*(3), 58-63.

Dimidjian, V.J. (1989). Holidays, holy days, and wholly dazed. *Young Children, 44*(6), 70-75.

(continued)

*To obtain a book published by NAEYC, call 800-424-2460 and ask for Resource Sales. For *Young Children* articles from the past five years, call the Institute for Scientific Information, 215-386-0100, ext. 5399, or fax 215-222-0840; from earlier issues, contact NAEYC's Public Affairs Department.

Dyson, A.H. (1988). Appreciate the drawing and dictating of young children. *Young Children, 43*(3), 25-32.

Enriching classroom diversity with books for children, in-depth discussion of them, and story-extension activities. *Young Children, 48*(3), 10-12.

Fauvre, M. (1988). Including young children with "new" chronic illnesses in an early childhood setting. *Young Children, 43*(6), 71-77.

Fox, R.A., Anderson, R.C., Fox, T.A., & Rodriguez, M.A. (1991). STAR parenting: A model for helping parents effectively deal with behavioral difficulties. *Young Children, 46*(6), 54-60.

Fox-Barnett, M., & Meyer, T. (1992). The teacher's playing at *my* house this week! *Young Children, 47*(5), 45-50.

Goldhaber, J. (1992). Sticky to dry; red to purple: Exploring transformation with play dough. *Young Children, 48*(1), 26-28.

Greenberg, P. (1986). Ideas that work with young children. Who has some good activities? *Young Children, 41*(2), 17-18.

Greenberg, P. (1987). Ideas that work with young children. Child choice—Another way to individualize—Another form of preventive discipline. *Young Children, 43*(1), 48-54.

Greenberg, P. (1987). Ideas that work with young children. Good discipline is, in large part, the result of a fantastic curriculum! *Young Children, 42*(3), 49-50.

Greenberg, P. (1988). Ideas that work with young children. Laughing all the way. *Young Children, 43*(2), 39-41.

Greenberg, P. (1988). Ideas that work with young children. Positive self-image: More than mirrors. *Young Children, 43*(4), 57-59.

Greenberg, P. (1988). Ideas that work with young children. The difficult child. *Young Children, 43*(5), 60-68.

Greenberg, P. (1988). Ideas that work with young children. Avoiding "me against you" discipline. *Young Children, 44*(1), 24-29.

Greenberg, P. (1990). Ideas that work with young children. Why not academic preschool? (Part 1). *Young Children, 45*(2), 70-80.

Greenberg, P. (1992). Why not academic preschool? (Part 2). Autocracy or democracy in the classroom? *Young Children, 47*(3), 54-64.

Greenberg, P. (1992). Ideas that work with young children. How to institute some simple democratic practices pertaining to respect, rights, roots, and responsibilities in any classroom (without losing your leadership position). *Young Children, 47*(5), 10-17.

Greenberg, P. (1993). Ideas that work with young children. How and why to teach all aspects of preschool and kindergarten math naturally, democratically, and effectively (for teachers who don't believe in academic programs, who do believe in educational excellence, and who find math boring to the max)—Part 1. *Young Children, 48*(4), 75-84.

Griffing, P. (1983). Encouraging dramatic play in early childhood. *Young Children, 38*(2), 13-22.
What teachers can do to involve children, how to arrange and equip play centers, and teacher's own involvement in play.

Gronlund, G. (1992). Coping with Ninja Turtle play in my kindergarten classroom. *Young Children, 48*(1), 21-25.

Haiman, P.E. (1991). Viewpoint. Developing a sense of wonder in young children: There is more to early childhood education than cognitive development. *Young Children, 46*(6), 52-53.

Hendrick, J. (1992). When does it all begin? Teaching the principles of democracy in the early years. *Young Children, 47*(3), 51-53.

Herrera, J.F., & Wooden, S.L. (1988). Some thoughts about effective parent-school communication. *Young Children, 43*(6), 78-80.

Hitz, R., & Driscoll, A. (1988). Praise or encouragement? New insights into praise: Implications for early childhood teachers. *Young Children, 43*(5), 6-13.

Holt, B-G. (1989). *Science with young children* (rev. ed.). Washington, DC: NAEYC.
This book will build *your* enthusiasm for science, as well as children's—it can be so simple!

Jalongo, M.R., & Collins, M. (1985). Singing with young children! Folk singing for nonmusicians. *Young Children, 40*(2), 17-22.
You can do it!

Karnes, M.B., Johnson, L.J., & Beauchamp, K.D.F. (1988). Enhancing essential relationships: Developing a nurturing affective environment for young children. *Young Children, 44*(1), 58-65.

Kelman, A. (1990). Choices for children. *Young Children, 45*(3), 42-45.

Kinsman, C.A., & Berk, L.E. (1979). Joining the block and housekeeping areas. Changes in play and social behavior. *Young Children, 35*(1), 66-75.
Helps reduce gender-separate play.

Kleckner, K.A., & Engel, R.E. (1988). A child begins school: Relieving anxiety with books. *Young Children, 43*(5), 14-18.

Knowler, K.A. (1988). Caregivers' corner. Orienting parents and volunteers to the classroom. *Young Children, 44*(1), 9.

Koeppel, J., & Mulrooney, M. (1992). The Sister Schools Program: A way for children to learn about cultural diversity—when there isn't any in their school. *Young Children, 48*(1), 44-47.

Kostelnik, M.J. (1992). Myths associated with developmentally appropriate programs. *Young Children, 47*(4), 17-23.

Kotloff, L.J. (1993). Fostering cooperative group spirit and individuality: Examples from a Japanese preschool. *Young Children, 48*(3), 17-23.

Lamme, L.L. (1979). Handwriting in an early childhood curriculum. *Young Children, 35*(1), 22-27.

Small-muscle development and eye-hand coordination activities in art and play activities prepare the child to write later.

Lamme, L.L., & McKinley, L. (1992). Creating a caring classroom with children's literature. *Young Children, 48*(1), 65-71.

Lanser, S., & McDonnell, L. (1991). Creating quality curriculum yet not buying out the store. *Young Children, 47*(1), 4-9.

Lasky, L., & Mukerji, R. (1980). *Art: Basic for young children.* Washington, DC: NAEYC.

MacCarry, B. (1989). More thoughts. . . . Helping preschool child care staff and parents do more with stories and related activities: A pilot joint venture between a Florida public library and local child care centers. *Young Children, 44*(2), 17-21.

MacIsaac, P., & King, S. (1989). What did you do with Sophie, teacher? *Young Children, 44*(2), 37-38.

How a teacher dealt with the death of a class pet.

Mavrogenes, N.A. (1990). Helping parents help their children become literate. *Young Children, 45*(4), 4-9.

McBride, B.A. (1989). Interaction, accessibility, and responsibility: A view of father involvement and how to encourage it. *Young Children, 44*(5), 13-19.

Miller, J. (1990). Three-year-olds in their reading corner. *Young Children, 46*(1), 51-54.

Mills, H., & Clyde, J.A. (1991). Children's success as readers and writers: It's the teacher's beliefs that make the difference. *Young Children, 46*(2), 54-59.

National Dance Association. (1991). *Early childhood creative arts.* Reston, VA: American Alliance for Health, Physical Education, Recreation and Dance.

Perry, G., & Rivkin, M. (1992). Teachers and science. *Young Children, 47*(4), 9-16.

Plourde, L. (1989). Teaching with collections. *Young Children, 44*(3), 78-80.

Poest, C.A., Williams, J.R., Witt, D.D., & Atwood, M.E. (1990). Challenge me to move: Large muscle development in young children. *Young Children, 45*(5), 4-10.

Read, K.H. (1992). The nursery school: A human relations laboratory. *Young Children, 47*(3), 4-5.

Great ideas to help with child guidance.

Rich, S.J. (1985). The writing suitcase. *Young Children, 40*(5), 42-44.

A good parent-involvement activity, as well as a good literacy-building activity.

Riley, S.S. (1984). *How to generate values in young children: Integrity, honesty, individuality, self-confidence, and wisdom.* Washington, DC: NAEYC.

Rivkin, M. (Ed.). Science is a way of life. *Young Children, 47*(4), 4-8.

Robinson, B.E. (1988). Vanishing breed: Men in child care programs. *Young Children, 43*(6), 54-58.

Schiller, M. (1995). An emergent art curriculum that fosters understanding. *Young Children, 50*(3), 33-38.

Schirrmacher, R. (1986). Talking with young children about their art. *Young Children, 41*(5), 3-7.

Sheldon, A. (1990). "Kings are royaler than queens": Language and socialization. *Young Children, 45*(3), 4-9.

Smith, C.A. (1979). Puppetry and problem-solving skills. *Young Children, 34*(3), 4-11.

Puppets help teachers gain entry into the child's world.

Spewock, T.S. (1992). Teaching parents of young children through learning packets. *Young Children, 47*(2), 28-30.

Stipek, D.J. (1983). Work habits begin in preschool. *Young Children, 38*(4), 25-32.

Attention to task and tasks that offer challenge, success as its own reinforcement, and use of informative praise.

Stone, J.G. (1978). *A guide to discipline* (rev. ed.). Washington, DC: NAEYC.

Strickland, D.S., & Morrow, L.M. (Eds.). (1989). *Emerging literacy: Young children learn to read and write.* Newark, DE: International Reading Association.

Sullivan, M. (1982). *Feeling strong, feeling free: Movement exploration for young children.* Washington, DC: NAEYC.

Suskind, D., & Kittel, J. (1989). Clocks, cameras, and chatter, chatter, chatter: Activity boxes as curriculum. *Young Children, 44*(2), 46-50.

Walton, S. (1989). Katy learns to read and write. *Young Children, 44*(5), 52-57.

Wardle, F. (1995). Alternatives . . . Bruderhof education: Outdoor school. *Young Children, 50*(3), 68-73.

Wolf, J. (1992). Let's sing it again: Creating music with young children. *Young Children, 47*(2), 56-61.

Wolter, D.L. (1992). Whole group story reading? *Young Children, 48*(1), 72-75.

Workman, S., & Anziano, M.C. (1993). Curriculum webs: Weaving connections from children to teachers. *Young Children, 48*(2), 4-9.

CHAPTER FIVE

School-Age Children

An effective program for school-age children (ages 5 to 12) complements rather than duplicates the school day by giving children opportunities to explore and build on their interests and skills. Program staff encourage children to play a meaningful role in program planning and operations so that the program reflects the ages, skills, and interests of the children enrolled. Children choose what they want to do, what materials they want to use, and with whom they want to play and work. They can relax and unwind, join a special interest club, play sports and games, and socialize with peers and adults. The primary role of staff is to facilitate children's involvement in games, clubs, sports, interest areas, and activities. They set up an interesting and challenging environment, provide materials, and plan special activities. Staff promote children's growing independence by encouraging them to solve their own problems, make and carry out their own plans, and become part of the community within the program and in the larger world beyond. This section offers information and guidance to help you oversee the environment, materials and equipment, program structure, activities and experiences, and supportive interactions of staff working with school-age children in center-based programs.

Environment _____

The school-age program environment includes the indoor and outdoor spaces regularly available to the children. Some programs have access to a gymnasium and other shared spaces, such as a dance studio, darkroom, kitchen, or swimming pool. Typically the environment is divided into interest areas—clearly defined spaces with materials and equipment focused on a specific type of activity. Interest areas offer children a wide range of choices to match individual and developmental skills and interests and to provide a balance between active and quiet experiences. Children can work and play alone or with a small group of friends. In a large space the areas can be relatively permanent, defined by architectural features and furniture. In smaller rooms some areas may remain in place throughout the year, while other areas are created in response to children's changing interests. Even programs that share space and must set up and take down each day can create interest areas by using rolling carts, baskets, or boxes to store and display materials. Ideally, children have access to an outdoor area adjacent to the indoor space. The outdoor environment also offers a range and variety of active and quiet activities. Children can make up games, play sports, climb and swing, skate and ride bikes, paint, read, eat snack, and work in a garden.

Environment (cont'd)

An appropriate environment for school-age children encourages all areas of development, allows children to make choices, supports children's growing independence, and offers opportunities to be alone and to socialize with others. Following are examples of what you should see in a program serving school-age children and why these arrangements of the environment are important.

What you should see	Why
a variety of interest areas (e.g., music, arts and crafts, woodworking), each including specific materials and equipment	Well-equipped areas can accommodate the wide range of skills and interests that school-age children are likely to bring to the program. Children can choose what they want to do and with whom, and they can find what they need to carry out their plans without having to ask staff for help or assistance.
individual, labeled spaces, such as cubbies or crates, in which children can store their school bags and other personal belongings	Children are more likely to take good care of their belongings and less likely to lose or misplace homework assignments if they have designated spaces to store materials before and after school. Children feel respected and secure when they know that their personal items are safe and "off-limits" to others without their permission. This avoids disagreements and misuse of belongings.
clearly defined indoor and outdoor traffic patterns and areas for active and quiet play	Children involved in active games and activities have plenty of room to play without getting in the way of children involved in quiet games and activities. Clear traffic patterns allow children to move from one area to another without disturbing games or works-in-progress.
private areas, such as two beanbag chairs in a corner, a pile of large pillows under the loft, and a small table with a single chair	Sometimes children want to play or work alone or just spend time with one or two others. They may need to relax, relieve stress, or take a break from the group to regain composure. Cozy, private areas also offer children a place to read, do homework, listen to music, daydream, or discuss the day's events with a friend.
unfinished projects safely stored on the top of tall shelves	School-age children may not have time to finish a project in one day or may get so involved that they work on it for many days or weeks. To be safe from harm, these projects should be stored out of other children's way.

SCHOOL-AGE CHILDREN

Sometimes children want to spend time alone to relax or take a break from the group.

Environment (cont'd)

What you should see	Why
an area reserved for use by the older children, who have arranged and decorated the space without adult assistance	Older children may feel as if they have outgrown the school-age program and may resent being grouped with children younger than they are. A special place, just for their use, acknowledges their growing independence and need to spend time with each other rather than with the staff and younger children.
materials, equipment, and cleaning supplies stored where children can reach and replace them	Children can find what they need to carry out their plans, feel independent because they can do things without adult help, and be responsible because they can clean up after themselves.
children's interests and accomplishments reflected in the program's displays and decorations	When children see their work displayed, they know their work is valued and take pride in their achievements. Items that respond to and extend their interests demonstrate respect for individuals and expose all children to new ideas and topics.
a safe, outdoor space where children can engage in a variety of games, sports, and activities that allow them to use their large muscles and where they can enjoy pursuits such as reading, thinking, painting, talking, woodworking, gardening, or eating snack	School-age children may arrive at the program with pent-up energy that needs to be expended after a day at school. Being outdoors gives children a sense of freedom not typically experienced during indoor play. In addition, the outdoors offers fresh air, new scenery, and a chance to experience nature.
space where children can spread out and make messes	Children are more likely to plan interesting and complex projects if they know they have plenty of room to work and that it's all right to make a mess, as long as they clean up afterwards.
space and materials adapted to provide appropriate experiences for children with disabilities	The environment should reflect the needs, skills, and interests of all children, including children with disabilities.
a parent bulletin board and area for sharing information about individual children, examples of children's work, an upcoming field trip, community activities of interest to families, opportunities to contribute to the program, and workshops on child development and parenting	Parents and staff are partners in identifying and responding to children's needs, skills, and interests. Parents are more likely to be meaningfully involved in the program if they feel welcome. A separate parent area encourages ongoing communication between parents and staff.

When the school-age program environment works well, children choose their own activities, enjoy being with friends at the program, and participate in program planning and operations. When the environment is not working, problem behaviors are likely to become the norm rather than the exception. You may observe children

- getting in the way of each other's play and projects;
- resisting cleanup;
- wandering around with nothing to do;
- waiting for staff to get them the things they need;
- misusing materials;
- losing their homework and personal belongings;
- shouting or talking in loud voices; or
- forming cliques and excluding others from the group.

There can be many different causes for behaviors such as these. However, in considering the reasons for children's misbehavior, it's a good idea to begin by looking at the environment. Listed below are warning signs that the environment might be inappropriate for school-age children, possible reasons why the environment is organized this way, and strategies you can try to help staff create a more effective environment.

Warning signs	Why this might be happening	How you can help
some interest areas seldom used by the children; other areas so crowded that the children complain of having no room to work	The staff created the interest areas without determining what the children want to do, or the materials in the interest areas have not been changed to reflect children's current skills and "passions."	Encourage staff to involve the children in planning the environment by conducting surveys, observing how children use the interest areas, and discussing as a group how to improve the interest areas. Suggest closing the unpopular areas, expanding the popular ones, and creating new ones, as appropriate.

When the environment is not working (cont'd)

Warning signs	Why this might be happening	How you can help
frequently chaotic departure for school in the morning and/or for home at the end of the day, with frustrated children unable to find their schoolwork and belongings	The spaces set aside for storing personal items are too small, or two or more children have to share a space rather than each child having an individual cubby or container.	Help staff rearrange the environment to make room for individual storage cubbies or containers. If necessary, obtain individual crates, lockers, or other storage units. Ask staff to make sure that personal spaces are labeled with children's names.
children frequently bickering with each other, getting into fights with little provocation, and easily losing their tempers	There are no spaces where children can get away from the group for a while to regain composure, relax and relieve stress, or spend time with a special friend.	Discuss with staff ways to create private spaces within the environment. Possibilities include an open carton lined with pillows, beanbag chairs that can be carried from one place to another, a comfortable chair, a small tent, and a sheet draped over a table.
children running or roaming outdoors without getting involved in activities	The staff view outdoor time as an opportunity for children to let off steam and make up their own games. Staff think they don't need to plan or provide materials and equipment for the outdoor environment.	While acknowledging that school-age children do need to let off steam and initiate their own games, point out that adults can provide guidance and materials to help children carry out their plans and introduce them to a wide variety of outdoor games and activities. Encourage staff to involve children in planning what to do outdoors and in selecting materials and equipment.

Warning signs	Why this might be happening	How you can help
children asking staff for assistance when selecting materials, asking where materials are located, and not putting things away when they are finished using them	Materials are stored out of children's reach, or the materials are stored so haphazardly that children can't find what they need.	Help staff work with the children to organize the program's shelves and storage units so that items used together are kept together and materials are easily accessible to all.
rushed drop-off and pick-up times, with parents and staff spending little time together	Staff may think parents are in a hurry to get to work in the morning and don't have time to talk, or the environment may not include a place that welcomes parents and facilitates communication.	Discuss the importance of keeping parents involved and informed—children spend many out-of-school hours at the program. Suggest involving children in creating a parent resource area. Children and staff can share the responsibility for keeping the area up-to-date (e.g., this week's schedule and menus, parenting magazines, photos from a field trip, donated items needed for a new interest area, and a sign-up sheet for a family picnic).
children running around indoors, engaging in horseplay and bumping into each other, causing many disagreements	The staff have arranged the room so that the furniture, equipment, and materials are lined up against the wall, leaving a wide-open space in the middle that invites children to run and expend physical energy.	Have staff use graph paper and paper scale models of furniture and equipment to redesign the room arrangement, then help them rearrange the room using the new design. Offer to observe children in the new environment and report your findings to the staff. Further adjustments can then be made if necessary.

Equipment and materials

The following "basic" interest areas are likely to be popular with most school-age children, ages 5 to 12. The suggested materials can encourage a wide range and variety of experiences and support all areas of growth and development. In addition, staff and children may want to create "sub-areas" within interest areas (for example, an inventions area within the science area) and smaller, temporary areas (for example, a "museum" with revolving displays of children's collections) that respond to current interests and are left up until children are ready to move on to other endeavors.

These lists are not all-inclusive; rather, they provide examples of the kinds of materials school-age children enjoy using. Share the lists with staff so they can use them as a resource when assessing and improving their program's materials and equipment.

Dramatic play

If younger children (5- to 7-year-olds) are enrolled in the program, a house corner will be well used. See Chapter 4 for a description of items to include. In addition, items such as the following will stimulate older children's interest in dramatic play.

- hooks or a clothes tree for hanging up costumes and dressup clothes
- costumes
- books of simple plays
- miscellaneous props
- puppets and supplies for making puppets
- puppet theater
- male and female dressup clothes, shoes, scarves, ties, hats, gloves
- suitcases, briefcases, purses
- jewelry
- household items (pots and pans, silverware, dishes, empty food containers)
- prop boxes related to specific themes (medical, travel agent, magic show, auto mechanic)
- props children can use to set up theme-related sub-areas (e.g., shopping mall, school, animal hospital)

Board and table games

- table and chairs
- materials for making games and puzzles
- puzzles of varying levels of complexity
- jacks
- Pick-up sticks
- crossword puzzles and word games
- playing cards (standard deck and specialized games)
- board games of varying levels of difficulty, such as Candyland, Chutes and Ladders, Sorry, Connect Four, Monopoly, Scrabble, trivia games, chess, checkers, and backgammon

Blocks and construction

- carpeted floor
- hardwood unit blocks (complete set)
- people props
  - multiethnic sets of families
  - multiethnic community helpers
- animal props
  - zoo animals
  - farm animals
- transportation props
  - cars, trucks, and other vehicles
  - traffic signs
- small blocks and construction sets (Legos, Bristle Blocks, Lincoln Logs)
- large hollow blocks

- sheets of cardboard or Tri-Wall board
- crates, large boxes, or appliance cartons
- sheets or large pieces of fabric for tents and clubhouses

Exploring math and science concepts

- table and chairs
- shelves for displays, an aquarium, pet cages, and storage
- source of light (preferably a sunny window)
- reference materials
- pegs and pegboards
- beads and laces
- colored inch-cube blocks
- Geo boards and colored rubber bands
- calculators
- rulers, yardsticks, measuring tapes, metersticks
- abacus
- parquetry blocks
- Attribute blocks
- Cuisenaire rods
- magnetic board and numbers
- hand lenses
- balance scales
- microscope and slides
- timers
- things to take apart (seeds, household items such as flashlights and pens, old clocks)
- tools for taking things apart (mallets, screwdrivers, pliers)
- ant farm
- aquarium
- bird feeders
- insect nets
- collection containers
- gardening supplies
- pets, cages, and supplies for their care
- plants
- materials for experiments
- thermometers
- magnets
- prisms and crystals

Woodworking

- workbench
- protective eye goggles
- carpenter aprons
- carpenter pencils
- soft wood (pine and balsa) for projects
- hardwood scraps
- dowel rods
- sandpaper
- tools (hammers, saws, hand drill and bits, screwdriver, pliers, vise, C-clamp)
- T square, rulers, and measuring tape
- screws and nails
- wood glue
- books with instructions for simple projects

Arts and crafts

- washable floor
- tables and chairs
- shelves
- easel (two-sided)
- paint (tempera, finger, and watercolor sets)
- brushes (variety of sizes and types)
- paper (easel, fingerpainting, construction, tissue, butcher, drawing)
- cardboard and poster board
- white and colored chalks
- crayons
- felt-tip markers (washable, nontoxic, broad and thin tips)
- scissors
- paper cutter
- stapler
- glue and rubber cement
- collage items
- yarn (different weights and textures)
- materials and tools for sculpting, modeling, and carving (playdough, clay)
- materials and tools for needlework (embroidery, crocheting, knitting, macramé, sewing, weaving)
- materials and tools for batik and tie-dye (dyes, basins, string, rubber bands, books, paraffin)

Equipment and materials (cont'd)

Quiet area

- carpeted floor
- table and chairs
- good source of light
- large pillows, beanbag chairs, or easy chair
- display shelves
- blackboard and chalk
- tape or CD player with headphones
- tapes or CDs (popular, ethnic, classical, jazz, folk, and traditional)
- books
  - showing a variety of ethnic groups
  - depicting men and women in varied roles
  - reflecting children's skills and interests
  - fiction and nonfiction
- reference materials
  - dictionaries
  - *Guinness Book of World Records*
  - *World Almanac*
  - maps (world, United States, state, local)
  - globe and/or atlases
  - books on topics of interest to children
- magazines on topics of interest to children
- newspapers
- writing supplies (paper, pens, pencils, erasers)
- bulletin board (maintained by children)
- posters and decorations (selected by children)
- computer and a variety of software

Sand and water

- washable floor
- sand/water table or basins
- waterproof aprons
- sponges and mops for cleanup
- props (e.g., hoses, pitchers, squeeze bottles, basters, tubing, sifters, shovels, funnels, boats, measuring cups)

Large group area

- carpeted floor for dancing and other physical activities
- table and chairs (for club meetings)
- storage space (for club supplies)
- loft with a ladder or large indoor climber

- supplies for indoor games and dancing (beanbags, foam balls, scarves, streamers, hula hoops, jump ropes)
- tape or CD player
- tapes or CDs
- musical instruments (homemade or purchased)

Outdoors and/or gymnasium

In addition to materials brought from the indoor environment, materials and equipment such as the following are available for use outdoors or in the gymnasium.

- safety equipment (helmets, knee and elbow pads)
- bats
- balls (playground and for specific sports)
- air pumps for balls
- street hockey sticks and pucks
- portable goal net
- badminton and volleyball equipment
- tennis rackets and balls
- cones to designate safe areas for different activities
- horseshoes
- balance beam
- hula hoops
- ring-toss sets
- individual jump ropes
- long ropes for jumping rope with a group
- chalk for hopscotch
- pogo sticks
- batons
- skates (roller and/or ice)
- sawhorses and boards
- large spools
- large cartons and crates
- water and sand play props
- hose and sprinklers
- items to use when playing in the snow (sleds, saucers, shovels, forms for making snow bricks)
- gardening tools and equipment
- shared items, such as swings, slides, climbers, climbing ropes, basketball hoops, a trampoline, tumbling mats

What you should see	**Why**
open-ended materials (e.g., a basket of fabric scraps, thread, and needles) and equipment (e.g., playground balls)	There is no right or wrong way to use open-ended materials. Children can decide what they want to make or do with these items and can use them in different ways, according to their interests, imagination, and skill level.
materials (e.g., board games) of varying levels of difficulty	School-age children represent a wide age range and, therefore, have varied skills and abilities. The program's materials should match the skills of the children enrolled and provide sufficient new challenges as children grow and develop.
materials and reference sources (books, magazines, computer programs) that allow children to pursue their special interests	School-age children want to learn more about the world beyond home and family. They may get fully involved in learning all they can about a specific topic (e.g., architecture) or want to develop a special skill or talent (photography). School-age programs should provide the materials that children need to explore these interests.
materials children can use to make "real" things	School-age children are interested in the tangible products of their efforts. They feel a sense of pride from creating things that have a purpose (e.g., a new board game, a pillow, a bird house, a play). They can make plans and have the physical and cognitive skills needed to carry them out.
materials (e.g., writing paper, pencils, computers, graph paper, calculators, measuring tools, books) that allow children to apply their rapidly growing reading, writing, arithmetic, thinking, and other skills	The school-age program complements rather than duplicates the school day by allowing children to use their skills in projects and activities of their own design and choosing. Children are more likely to become lifelong learners if they can use their academic skills in ways that are meaningful to them (e.g., reading a book for pleasure rather than because it is a school assignment).

In school-age programs, children benefit from a wide variety of experiences, including arts and crafts, cooking, dramatics, nature study, and music.

Equipment and materials (cont'd)_____

What you should see	**Why**
materials (e.g., props and costumes, art and craft supplies, a computer and writing program, "raw" materials for science experiments, a tape player and blank tapes) that encourage children's creativity	School-age children can use all their skills—physical, socioemotional, language, and cognitive—in creative pursuits. They may have special talents and interests they want to explore in creative ways. Providing a wide variety of interesting materials in the environment encourages children to explore, experiment, express their ideas, and carry out their plans.
materials that provide children with a wide variety of experiences (e.g., music and movement, sports and games, arts and crafts, building, nature study, cooking, dramatics)	Children need a broad range of experiences to develop in all domains—cognitively, socioemotionally, and physically.
materials (e.g., puppets, books, posters, magazines, props) that reflect diverse ethnic and cultural backgrounds and do not present biases based on gender or other characteristics	Children learn to feel good about themselves and others when they see a variety of cultures and ethnicities reflected in the program's materials. They are defining what it means to be male or female in our culture and need exposure to a full range of roles for men and women. As they learn more about the world beyond home and family, they are eager to learn about other people—what they have in common and how they are unique.
materials (e.g., balls, jump ropes, stop-watches, hula hoops, skates) that encourage participation in individual and group physical activities	School-age children are developing fitness habits they may carry with them into adulthood. Some children enjoy group games and sports, such as softball or basketball. Other children prefer activities such as jogging, jumping rope, or aerobics. The program should offer a variety of equipment so that children can choose physical activities that match their skills and interests.

When equipment and materials are inappropriate

During your visits to the program, children may seem bored and uninvolved or staff might complain of behavior problems. If so, the problem may lie with the equipment and materials. Because children's skills and interests are constantly changing, the program's materials should be regularly updated to provide new challenges and to build on current "passions." If you observe warning signs such as the ones that follow, encourage staff to work with the children to assess the equipment and materials included in each interest area, then help them make the necessary changes.

Warning signs	Why this might be happening	How you can help
children using the same materials day after day in routine ways	Children may be repeating activities (e.g., playing chess) to master them or because it is the latest popular activity (e.g., drawing cartoons); the materials may be too challenging or not challenging enough; children may be overlooking materials because they don't know what is available or don't know how to use some materials.	Ask staff to observe children to determine whether they are repeating activities to master a skill or because it is the current "craze." If the observations show that the children are not gaining anything from repeated use of the same materials, suggest rearranging seldom-used materials to make them more prominent and demonstrating how to use them.
the same materials available each day and throughout the year	Staff are not changing the inventory to respond to children's changing interests and growing skills. They may think that the children have plenty to choose from and enjoy having familiar items available, or that the program can purchase items only once a year.	Suggest that staff survey children several times a year to find out what materials they would like to have at the program. In addition, encourage staff to regularly observe children to see what materials they are using and what might be added to the inventory to build upon their interests and skills. Encourage use of recycled items, books and tapes from the library, and donations from parents and the community. Make sure the program's system for purchasing materials allows for replacing and enhancing the inventory several times a year so that it matches children's current interests and skills.

Warning signs	Why this might be happening	How you can help
most of the children participating in one type of activity (e.g., arts and crafts or softball) while the rest mill around with nothing to do	The program does not have a wide variety of materials to encourage different kinds of activities. Staff may think that all children will want to do the same thing—play ball, paint, learn a song.	Lead a workshop on what school-age children are like, their different needs and interests, and their desire to choose what they want to do during out-of-school time. Suggest that staff meet with small groups of children to discuss what they would like to do at the program and what materials they need for these activities.
children accusing each other of cheating during board games	The program may be emphasizing competition rather than having a good time playing the games, or the games may be too difficult for the children enrolled, or they may not understand the rules.	Help staff assess the program climate to make sure that it doesn't overemphasize winning and losing. Remind staff that children who have difficulty losing may be at a stage in their development when losing a game feels like an intense personal loss. Such children need staff assistance to get involved in less-competitive activities. Also, ask staff to review the inventory of board games to make sure they are appropriate for the ages and skills of the children enrolled. Suggest that staff offer to review the rules with children, play with them until the players understand, and model enjoyment of the game.

When equipment and materials are inappropriate (con't) ————

Warning signs	Why this might be happening	How you can help
children using coloring books, baking mixes, or craft kits	Staff want the children to feel successful, so they provide pre-packaged, one-dimensional activities that result in products children can take home. They may think pre-packaged kits are good learning tools. They don't realize these activities thwart rather than encourage creativity.	Offer a hands-on workshop that models using open-ended materials to encourage use of imagination and creativity. Have half the group use pre-packaged kits with specific instructions to make something (e.g., a pot-holder) while the other half uses open-ended materials to make the same product. Ask the two groups to compare what they did to make the product. Point out what children (and adults) gain from developing designs and plans, choosing materials, experimenting with techniques, and so on, versus what they gain from following someone else's design, plans, choice of color and materials, and so on.
children misusing or breaking the program's materials	Materials may be too challenging or not challenging enough; materials may be too flimsy for use by groups of children; or there is no logical system for storing and protecting materials. Staff may have selected items without children's input, so the children don't feel a sense of ownership and responsibility for taking care of the program's materials.	Suggest that staff hold a group meeting to discuss the problem, and involve children in setting a few simple rules about taking care of the materials. In addition, help staff review the program's inventory to make sure the materials provide sufficient challenge without causing frustration. At the same time, look for items that can't stand up to daily use by a group of children (e.g., rubber play-ground balls will last longer than plastic ones), and plan to replace these materials as soon as possible. Finally, if your observations indicate that the storage system is not working, photograph children having difficulty putting away materi-als. Share the pictures with staff, and have them involve the children in rearranging the system so it encourages cleanup instead of misuse of materials.

Program structure: Schedule and routines

The program structure in a school-age program should be more flexible than the program at school, where certain lessons have to be covered within a set period of time. At the school-age program, children can choose what they want to do, what materials they want to use, and with whom they would like to work and play. An appropriate schedule includes long blocks of time when children can be fully involved in their work and play without being interrupted. There is time for outdoor and indoor play, children can be alone or part of a small or large group, there is a balance between active and quiet experiences, and children are encouraged to be independent. In addition, the schedule should provide sufficient time for routines, such as eating breakfast; making transitions from the program to school and vice versa; and doing chores, such as cleaning pet cages, that keep the program operating smoothly. Although children clean up as they finish a game or project (e.g., by putting away the pieces to a board game or returning the street hockey equipment to the storage shed), the schedule also includes time for cleaning up activities and interest areas, storing outdoor equipment, and gathering belongings at the end of morning, afternoon, and full-day sessions.

Sample Schedule for a School-Age Program

Before School

6:30-7:00 A.M.	Children arrive, a few interest areas are open for quiet activities, and staff and children get ready for breakfast.
7:00-7:30	Breakfast is served; children who aren't eating continue quiet activities.
7:30-8:10	All interest areas are open. In addition, staff lead short-term, quiet activities that don't require a lot of setup, can be saved if not completed, or will be completed during the afternoon session.
8:10-8:25	Children clean up activities and interest areas and get ready for school.
8:25-8:30	Children leave for school (walkers and bus riders).
8:30-9:30	Staff meeting, planning time, and/or professional development.

Program structure: Schedule and routines (cont'd)

After Kindergarten—Early Afternoon

12:00-12:30 P.M. Kindergarten children arrive after morning session, wash hands, eat lunch family style.

12:30-1:00 Storytime.

1:00-2:00 Rests, naps, or quiet activities (depending on each child's needs).

2:00-2:10 Transition—children pick up activities or get up from resting.

2:10-2:40 Interest areas are open. Staff oversee short-term activities.

2:40-3:00 Group time—children sing songs, share, discuss activities planned for the rest of the afternoon.

After School

3:00-3:30 Children arrive. A staff member does a visual attendance check. Children get their snacks from a self-service area.

3:30-3:45 (4:00 if group meeting) Group meeting time (daily, weekly, or as needed). Children move to activities, interest areas, or outdoors.

3:45-5:30 Children use the interest areas or participate in activities of their choice.

5:30-5:45 Some interest areas close for the day. Children clean up, store projects in progress, gather belongings and projects they want to take home.

5:45-6:30 Some interest areas (e.g., science and nature, board games, quiet area, large-group activity area) remain open. A staff member greets parents and helps them find their children.

What you should see	**Why**
children taking care of personal routines (using the bathroom, eating, relaxing) according to individual schedules	Children have different temperaments and bodily needs. Allowing children to eat, use the bathroom, and relax when they feel the need demonstrates respect for them as individuals.
long blocks of time when children choose what they want to do	Most of the time children spend at the program, they should be able to choose what they want to do. After spending a day in school, with required tasks and assignments, they are ready to be independent, select materials and activities, and make and carry out plans. Long blocks of time allow them to carry out plans without interruption.
snack set up in a self-service area	Some children are so hungry that they are ready for snack as soon as they arrive at the program; others need to spend some time unwinding before sitting down to eat. A self-service snack area allows children to choose when and how much they want to eat.
sufficient time for children to clean up and store their work at the end of morning, afternoon, and full-day sessions	School-age children are able to assume responsibility for taking care of the program environment. When time is included in the schedule for cleanup, children can work together to keep the program running smoothly.
some activities planned and led by adults	Staff-led activities are an appropriate part of a school-age program as long as children can choose whether they want to participate. Children may ask staff to help them plan and carry out a specific activity, or staff may plan an activity they think will be fun or interesting or will help children learn a specific skill. Some children enjoy working with and learning from a particular adult.

Program structure: Schedule and routines (cont'd) ___

What you should see	Why
arrival and departure times used as opportunities to share with parents	The time children spend at the school-age program is a significant part of their day. Parents and staff need time to talk about what children are doing and how to coordinate children's home, program, school, and community experiences.
a balance between active and quiet activities	Most school-age children need to engage in active play; however, it is also important to offer quiet activities that provide a change of pace and allow children to recoup their energy.
daily outdoor play opportunities (weather permitting)	The children enrolled in a school-age program may have few opportunities to play outdoors because they get home too late or because their neighborhoods are unsafe. The daily outdoor play offered at the school-age program may be the only time children can enjoy the feeling of freedom that comes from being outdoors.
children doing long-term projects	Many school-age children have the interest and attention span to do long-term projects that last several days or weeks and allow them to fully explore an interest, express creativity, or master a skill.
staff and children meeting as a group when needed	Group meetings are times when children can be involved in planning, solving problems, or listening to a guest speaker. In addition, they give children a sense of community within the program.

When the program structure is not working _____

During your visits to the school-age program, you may observe high levels of stress and frustration in children and staff. Staff may struggle to maintain control; children may resist being told what to do and refuse to cooperate. If you see warning signs such as the following, review the possible causes, then help staff make the needed changes in the program's schedule and procedures for completing routines.

Warning signs	Why this might be happening	How you can help
staff cleaning up after the children leave	Cleanup time is not included in the schedule, so children don't participate in cleanup as a regular part of their time at the program.	Have staff revise the schedule to include time for cleanup before children leave for school and at the end of the day. Discuss how to implement the new schedule so that cleanup responsibilities are shared with children.
all children eating snack or meals at the same time	Staff find it more convenient to have everyone eat at the same time. They don't recognize the importance of accommodating children's differing temperaments and bodily needs.	Work with staff to create a self-service snack area. Identify a place to set it up, discuss how to serve the food, and determine how to involve children in planning, serving, and cleaning up.
staff interrupting children so they can participate in a staff-planned group activity	Staff may think the activity they planned is a more interesting and appropriate experience for the children, or they have something special to share. They may want all the children to benefit from doing the activity.	Remind staff of the importance of allowing children to choose their own activities and materials. Staff-planned activities may be fun and interesting; however, children should be able to choose not to participate. Suggest offering activities more than once so children have several chances to participate.

Because many children today have few opportunities to play outside, school-age programs need to offer daily outdoor play when weather permits.

Warning signs	Why this might be happening	How you can help
most of the children participating in group activities	Staff may think they are offering choices because then children can decide which group activity to join.	Help staff create an environment and schedule that encourage child choice and provide a balance between individual, small-group, and large-group activities and experiences. Explain that group activities can be one option in a high-quality program as long as they aren't the only option available to children.
staff telling children they have to stop working on their projects even though the session hasn't ended	Staff think that children need a rigid schedule so they will learn to budget their time. The schedule doesn't include enough time for children to carry out their plans.	Help staff understand that school-age children enjoy and benefit from sticking with a project for a long period of time. Ask staff to think about how they feel when asked to hurry up and finish a project before they are ready to declare it finished. Have staff look at their schedule to make sure it gives children plenty of time to carry out their plans.
children appearing exhausted or sitting around doing nothing at the end of the day	Children are overtired, perhaps because the schedule does not allow for alternate periods of active and quiet play and does not include a transition from active play to winding down to get ready to go home.	Review the schedule with staff, and plan ways to provide a better balance so the end of the day is a calm and relaxed time. Suggest offering active pursuits earlier in the day so children will have ample time to recoup their energy.

Activities and experiences

School-age programs serve children with a wide range of ages, skill levels, and interests. It is an enormous challenge to provide activities and experiences for a group that spans the period from early childhood, to middle childhood, to preadolescence, to early adolescence. Balance is a key feature in effective programs. Activities and experiences include those that are active and quiet; take place indoors and outdoors; involve individuals and small and large groups; are child initiated and planned and led by staff; and allow children to use cognitive, physical, and socioemotional skills. Children can spend time with peers of their own age or participate in activities with children younger and older than they are. There are opportunities for cooperation and competition. Children can use and expand their skills and learn to do things they've never tried before. Staff encourage children to explore their special interests and expose them to new topics that might lead to new interests. Listed below are examples of the types of activities and experiences you should be overseeing during your visits to programs and why they enhance children's growth and development.

What you should see	Why
children using social skills (e.g., older children helping younger ones, resolving their own disagreements, making up and playing games, helping a friend study for a test, leading a club meeting) as they participate in the program	Through many interactions with peers and adults, children develop social skills and learn to understand themselves. School-age children tend to base their opinions of themselves on their perceptions of how others view them. Peers are all-important, so children need many opportunities to play and cooperate with each other.
children using their large muscle skills (e.g., shooting baskets, jogging around the field, playing soccer, dancing, playing hopscotch)	Physical activities allow children to expend energy, feel competent, and develop fitness habits that may last into adulthood.
children using their small-muscle skills (e.g., sewing puppets, typing on a computer keyboard, kneading bread, painting with watercolors, building with Legos)	School-age children like to do and make real things. Their increasing small-muscle skills and eye-hand coordination allow them to use tools (e.g., paintbrushes, needles, scissors, crochet hooks) with control and proficiency.
children using their cognitive skills (e.g., reading, writing to a pen pal, displaying a rock collection, doing experiments, doing homework, learning a new computer program)	School-age children can reason logically, approach problems systematically, order and organize things by properties, and pursue special interests and hobbies. They can use the academic skills learned in school to carry out plans of their own.

What you should see

children exploring their creativity (e.g., writing and illustrating a poem, designing costumes for a play, building a clubhouse, drawing on the blacktop with chalk, making up a dance routine)

children leaving the program to attend community activities (e.g., soccer practice, scouts, or a gymnastics class), serve as volunteers (e.g., on a road cleanup crew or in the children's ward at a hospital), or go on a field trip (e.g., to a park, museum, or behind-the-scenes tour of a business)

staff asking children open-ended questions (e.g., What might happen if . . . ? What other ways could you use . . . ?)

children making and carrying out plans without adult assistance

children holding meetings of clubs focused on a shared interest (e.g., newspaper, gardening, kite, cooking, or environment clubs)

Why

Most children enter the school-age years as eager learners, naturally imaginative and creative. The school-age program can encourage children's creativity and let them know that their ideas and creations are valued. When creativity is encouraged, children are likely to stay interested in learning, take risks, and try out ideas, even if they are not always successful.

Involving children in community activities as participants or volunteers helps them to feel connected to the world beyond home, school, and the program. Playing on teams and attending scouts or specialty classes allows children to pursue interests and increase their skills. Field trips expose them to new subjects and ideas.

Open-ended questions help children develop creative thinking and problem-solving skills, which they can apply in many life and learning situations.

There is probably nothing more satisfying for children than doing things for themselves. After a day in school, where most activities are planned and led by adults, children are ready to use their thinking skills to make their own plans, individually or with their peers.

Sponsoring clubs at the school-age program gives children of like interests a chance to explore them together and learn from each other. Clubs can be organized around almost anything of interest to a small group of children. Children can take the lead in planning and holding meetings, while staff respond to requests for materials and assistance.

When the activities are inappropriate

Despite the good intentions and plans of program staff, sometimes the activities and experiences do not result in a balanced program of activities and experiences. If you see warning signs such as the ones that follow, review the possible causes and help staff redesign the program so it offers children a range of appropriate activity choices.

Warning signs	Why this might be happening	How you can help
children spending *most* of their time doing homework or activities focused on intellectual growth	Staff are responding to parental requests that children finish all of their homework before doing anything else, or staff believe that children will do better in school if they focus on using academic skills.	Help staff review the program philosophy and commitment to providing a variety of out-of-school activities from which children can choose. Role play ways to discuss homework with parents—perhaps children can unwind and play for a while, then begin their homework. Introduce staff to Howard Gardner's theories on multiple intelligences, and suggest ways to provide materials and experiences that allow children to use different kinds of talents.
staff completing children's projects for them (e.g., sewing up the opening in a pillow, taking muffins out of the oven, or looking up words in the dictionary)	Staff think they are being helpful and supporting children. They don't want children to become frustrated and stop trying. They think that children want to be helped rather than do things for themselves.	Ask staff to think about how they might feel (frustrated? annoyed? incompetent?) if someone helped them complete a task without being asked. Explain that children develop a sense of competence by doing things for themselves. When staff help a child without being asked, they take away the child's good feelings about accomplishing something difficult or persevering even when things don't go as planned.

Warning signs	Why this might be happening	How you can help
children in one age group busy playing and working, while children in another age group are wandering with nothing to do	Staff have not provided a sufficent range of materials and activities for the varied ages and abilities of children present in the program.	Have staff meet with the children in the affected age group to find out what kinds of materials or activities they would like at the program. Encourage staff to conduct regular observations so they can keep track of when the program is not meeting children's needs.
older children complaining that they are too old for the program	Staff may have neglected to plan with the specific needs of the older children in mind. They may agree with the older children and think there is nothing staff can do to keep them interested.	Plan a workshop on the developmental characteristics of older school-age children (usually, 11- and 12-year-olds) and the types of activities they are likely to enjoy. Have staff meet with the children to discuss what they wish they were doing instead of coming to the program. Staff can acknowledge these "wishes" by trying to accommodate them in some way at the program. For example, children might say they wish they could watch soap operas. Staff can explain that watching television is not a program activity, but they can provide materials, space, and time for children to write and perform their own soap operas.
all children doing the same activities at the same time	Staff may think this is a good way to keep the program well organized and the children supervised and under control.	Review with staff the two components of a developmentally appropriate program— meeting individual and developmental needs. Explain that it's not possible to meet individual or developmental needs when all children do the same thing at the same time. Point out that when children choose their own activities, they are less likely to misbehave because of frustration or boredom.

Warning signs	Why this might be happening	How you can help
all children spending *most* of their time playing group games or sports	Staff think that children need plenty of time to be physically active after a sedentary day in school. They may think that all children would rather play games and sports than participate in any other activities.	Have staff survey the children to find out what they would like to do during their out-of-school hours. Help staff plan and implement a variety of activities that encourage all areas of development, reflect children's interests, and offer children choices.

Supportive interactions _____

School-age children are eager to make choices, be independent, assume responsibility, and plan and carry out their own projects. When children are happily involved in their own play and projects, it may seem that they don't need much time or attention from the program staff. However, the supportive interactions between program staff and children are the "fuel" that helps children accomplish their goals. Staff are there to step in when children request their assistance or when they see that their involvement will help children overcome an obstacle or resolve a disagreement that has gotten out of hand. Through ongoing, systematic observations, staff identify children who need help gaining social skills, making friends, or joining in an activity. They encourage children's positive interactions with each other, ask questions that stimulate creativity and thinking, provide opportunities for children to contribute to the program community, listen to children and respond to their concerns, help children develop self-discipline, and encourage cooperation and leadership. In a school-age program where the human interactions are supportive, each child and each adult is a valued member of the community.

What you should see	Why
staff and children working together to make decisions about the program, including rules and guidelines for behavior	The program is more likely to reflect children's interests if the children are involved in the planning process. Children feel a sense of ownership and belonging when they help make decisions about the program. Children tend to understand the reasons for rules and be more willing to follow them if they are involved in setting the rules.

Supportive interactions (cont'd) _____

What you should see	**Why**
staff listening and responding to children's concerns and adopting their suggestions when appropriate	Children feel valued when they can voice their concerns, even if staff cannot change the program to accommodate them. For example, children might want to bring their bikes to the program. If the program has nowhere to store them safely, this request cannot be met; but staff might plan a biking trip for a school vacation day. Children's suggestions are often more innovative than those that the adults come up with. Adults' adopting these suggestions helps children feel competent.
staff encouraging children to try out their ideas and helping them try again when their projects and experiments don't work out as planned	Trial and error is one of the most effective ways for children to express their creativity and learn about the world. Staff can help children accept mistakes as a natural part of life and encourage them to try again with new plans and ideas.
children and staff appreciating and showing respect for each person's unique characteristics and talents	Each child and each adult is a unique human being. When staff recognize and encourage children's unique characteristics, the staff help children feel good about what makes them special. They also model respect for diversity, which helps children to accept themselves and others.
children playing some games that encourage cooperation rather than competition	Some children enjoy and benefit from competition; some do not. The school-age program can introduce children to games and activities that encourage cooperation rather than competition and allow them to have fun and learn new skills without worrying about winning or losing.
staff welcoming parents to the program and sharing information about children's activities, interests, and experiences	Parents and staff are partners in helping children have fun and make good use of their out-of-school time. The information that each "partner" shares helps to make the school-age program appropriate for all the children enrolled.

When interactions are inappropriate

If you visit a program where children and staff seem tense and unhappy, as though they can't wait for the day to end; children are disrespectful of each other and of adults; and staff treat all the children in the same way, with little regard for individual strengths and characteristics, there may be problems related to a lack of supportive interactions. If you see warning signs such as the following, children may not be receiving the support they need from staff. Review the possible reasons why this might be happening, then work with staff to help make the program's social climate one that supports children and encourages their independence, responsibility, and sense of community.

Warning signs	Why this might be happening	How you can help
staff showing favoritism to some children while ignoring others	Liking some children more than others, which is a natural tendency, staff do not realize that they are failing to give all children equal time and attention.	Help staff understand their commitment to supporting the growth and development of all the children in the program. Discuss appropriate ways to deal with neutral or negative feelings about individual children. Also, point out how preferential, inconsistent behavior makes all the children feel insecure—they may think that if one child can be overlooked, then so can they.
staff immediately and publicly correcting children's behavior, without considering the reasons behind the behavior or helping the child learn self-discipline	Staff may want to make an "example" of the child to prevent further incidents. In addition, staff may believe that the consequences of misbehavior should be the same, regardless of the child involved and the cause of the problem behavior.	Hold a workshop on the differences between punishment and discipline and why it is important to help children learn to control their own behavior—a skill they will use now and in the future. Ask staff to think of the ways in which they use self-discipline in their own lives, so they can view it as a valuable lifelong skill. Discuss positive guidance techniques that encourage appropriate behavior without punishing children or causing them to feel bad about themselves.

Warning signs	Why this might be happening	How you can help
staff shouting or yelling at children to get their attention	Staff think this is the best way to get all the children to listen at the same time. Staff don't realize that when some children hear loud voices and yelling, they tune them out rather than listening to the message. Staff may think it's OK to yell at children, even though they know it would be disrespectful to yell at adults. Staff may yell from a distance outdoors, rather than walking to where the children are playing.	Have staff tape-record the program for an hour or two, then listen to their interactions with children. Ask, "Are you talking to children in ways you would want someone to talk to you?" Ask staff to make a commitment to use other means to get children's attention (e.g., dimming the lights, playing a tune on the xylophone, or turning on a specific piece of music).
staff making up new rules on the spot without involving children or explaining why the rules are needed	Staff may think it is all-important to remain in control of the group. They may believe that staff need to set rules to assert their authority.	Acknowledge that it may take more time to involve children in setting rules; however, the benefits are great. Ask staff to consider how they feel when rules that affect their lives are changed without their input or involvement or any explanation of why the changes are needed. Ask, "Are you more likely to understand and follow rules that you help set or those that are imposed on you?"
staff publicly reprimanding or making fun of children for their failures or mistakes	Staff don't realize the harm they are doing to children's feelings of competence and self-esteem. Staff may think that teasing is harmless and will help children laugh about their setbacks. Staff don't realize that making fun of children's mistakes can cause children to give up and not try again in the future.	During visits to the program, model ways to help children learn from their mistakes and to encourage them to try again. Help staff understand that most great inventions result from trial and error, taking risks, and learning from mistakes. Again, ask staff to consider how they feel when someone makes fun of their mistakes. Ask, "Does it make you want to try again, or does it make you want to give up?"

By responding to children's spontaneous interests, staff enhance learning and development.

When interactions are inappropriate (cont'd)_____

Warning signs	Why this might be happening	How you can help
staff telling children what to do, when, and with whom	Staff think children need to be directed to be productively involved in activities and to stay out of trouble.	Emphasize with staff the primary role for adults in school-age programs—as a facilitator of children's learning and development. Explain that facilitators create the environment, plan and introduce activities, provide opportunities to learn new skills, explain the rules in games, ask stimulating questions, and guide children's participation. Explain the benefits of operating a program based on child choice: children are less dependent on staff and more able to use their inner resources and abilities. This frees staff to assist those children who really do need more adult attention.
staff ignoring parents or speaking to them curtly	Staff may know how to work with children but have little experience communicating with adults. They may think it's only necessary to talk to parents when there is a problem or when they need something for the program.	Help staff plan a family event, such as a picnic or talent show, so they can get to know parents in a relaxed atmosphere. The children can help plan and get ready for the event. Review the different roles that parents and staff play in children's lives. Help staff understand that effective communication with parents makes their jobs easier and the program more effective for children.

Resources for working with school-age programs

Albrecht, K., & Plantz, M. (1991). *Developmentally appropriate practice in school-age child care* and (1991) *Quality criteria for school-age child care programs.* Alexandria, VA: Project Home Safe, American Home Economics Association.

These two resources describe appropriate practice and operations in school-age programs.

Albrecht, K., & Plantz, M. (1993). *Tools for schools: Contracting for school-age child care.* Alexandria, VA: Project Home Safe, American Home Economics Association.

A guide for school administrators who are looking for a contractor to operate school-age programs.

Bender, J., Elder, B., & Flatter, C.H. (1984). *Half a childhood: Time for school-age child care.* Nashville, TN: School-Age NOTES.

A broad overview of what school-age children are like, how programs can meet their needs, and suggested equipment and materials, activities, and schedules. Appendixes address the needs of children at both ends of the age spectrum—5-year-olds and 12-year-olds.

Bergstrom, J. (1990). *All the best contests for kids.* Berkeley, CA: Ten Speed Press.

One hundred twenty contests for children between the ages of 6 and 12. Interested children can demonstrate their skills in photography, writing, jumping rope, dancing, art, sewing, and computers.

Click, P. (1994). *Caring for school-age children.* Albany, NY: Delmar.

This book is for staff who work with school-age children. There are chapters on how children grow and develop, budgeting, planning, and the environment. Section 2 addresses all aspects of the curriculum. The final section of the book discusses the community and how to involve representatives in the program.

Fink, D. (1988). *School-age children with special needs: What do they do when school is out?* Boston: Exceptional Parent Press.

This book discusses the child care needs of school-age children with disabilities and offers suggestions for meeting these needs.

Gardner, H. (1993). *Multiple intelligences: The theory in practice.* New York: Basic.

Gardner explains his theory of multiple intelligences and describes how to apply the theories to help children develop to their full potential.

Greenspan, S. (1993). *Playground politics.* Reading, MA: Addison-Wesley.

Dr. Greenspan reviews the stages of normal emotional development for children in the school-age years and offers suggestions on how to assist children in handling typical problems and challenges.

Haas-Foletta, K., & Cogley, M. (1990). *School-age ideas and activities for after school programs.* Nashville, TN: School-Age NOTES.

Helpful hints and strategies, with more than 140 program-tested activities and games. There are ideas on shared space, scheduling, programming for older children, clubs, summer themes, and field trips.

Koralek, D.G., Newman, R., & Colker, L.J. (1995). *Caring for children in school-age programs.* Washington, DC: Teaching Strategies.

A comprehensive, self-instructional training program in two volumes for staff in school-age programs. Content and skills addressed reflect quality standards for school-age care as defined by national school-age professional groups and experts. Also available is a trainer's guide that explains how to implement and oversee the training program and assist staff in assessing their progress.

Kreidler, W.J. (1984). *Creative conflict resolution: More than 200 activities for keeping peace in the classroom K-6.* Glenview, IL: Scott, Foresman.

Conflict-resolution techniques, activities, and cooperative games for school-age children. Practical strategies to help children improve their communication skills, understand and settle their own disputes, and deal with strong feelings in productive ways.

Kreidler, W.J., & Furlong, L. (1996). *Adventures in peacemaking: A conflict resolution activity guide for school-age programs.* Cambridge, MA: Educators for Social Responsibility.

Provides a variety of activities designed to teach school-age children how to use conflict resolution to solve problems and disagreements.

Musson, S. (1993). *School-age care: Theory and practice.* Reading, MA: Addison Wesley.

This guide connects theories—what children in this age group need—and practice—how a school-age program can plan and implement a diverse array of activities and approaches to meet these needs.

National Association of Elementary School Principals and Wellesley School-Age Child Care Project. (1993). *Standards for quality school-age child care.* Alexandria, VA: National Association of Elementary School Principals.

Provides standards of excellence and quality indicators for a number of program elements, including staff–child relationships, staff–parent relationships, developmental programming, materials, equipment, and supplies. Appendixes include a checklist for applying the standards and a bibliography for further reading.

O'Connor, S.O. (1994). *Assessing school-age child care quality.* Wellesley, MA: School-Age Child Care Project, Wellesley College.

Guides school-age programs through assessments of all aspects of program operations. Implementation involves a team of staff, parents, children, and community members working together to evaluate their programs and develop and implement a plan for program improvement.

O'Connor, S., Harms, T., Cryer, D., & Wheeler, K. (1994). *Assessing school-age child care quality: Program observation and questions for the director.* Wellesley, MA: School-Age Child Care Project, Wellesley College.

This pair of observation and interview instruments can be used by school-age programs to complete a 10-step self-assessment process to guide improvement

Sisson, L.G. (1990). *Kids club: A school-age program guide for directors.* Nashville, TN: School-Age NOTES.

Provides basic information on how to operate a child-centered school-age program. Topics include the environment, activities, routines, field trips, supervision, parent communication, and resources.

Further resources from NAEYC*

Alexander, N.P. (1986). School-age child care: Concerns and challenges. *Young Children, 42*(1), 3–10.

Blakley, B., Blau, R., Brady, E.H., Streibert, C., Zavitkovsky, A., & Zavitkovsky, D. (1989). *Activities for school-age child care.* Washington, DC: NAEYC.

This resource includes hundreds of activities for children ages 5 through 10. Suggestions for working with parents are included.

McCracken, J.B. (1993). *Valuing diversity: The primary years.* Washington, DC: NAEYC.

Helps staff recognize how materials and activities in the program reflect the valuing (or devaluing) of diversity.

Powell, D.R. (1987). Research in review. After-school child care. *Young Children, 42*(3), 62–66.

*To obtain a book published by NAEYC, call 800-424-2460 and ask for Resource Sales. For *Young Children* articles from the past five years, call the Institute for Scientific Information, 215-386-0100, ext. 5399, or fax 215-222-0840; from earlier issues, contact NAEYC's Public Affairs Department.

CHAPTER SIX

Family Child Care

Family child care is well suited to the philosophy behind developmental programming. Because of the structure of family child care, every child is always in the forefront. This structure also allows providers to get to know children well: their likes and dislikes, their hopes and fears, their interests and passions. Providers use this information to create programs that help the children in their care grow and develop to the fullest.

Providers who offer high-quality care overcome a number of challenges. They create effective learning environments despite limits caused by the physical layouts of homes. Without expending large sums of money, they stock their homes with a wide range of toys and equipment to meet the needs of a multi-age group. They develop and use schedules that meet the needs of children of many ages and stages.

This chapter offers information and guidance to help you oversee the environment, materials and equipment, program structure, activities and experiences, and supportive interactions of family child care providers.

Environment

In an effective family child care program, the provider arranges her home to facilitate children's growth and development, while retaining the warm, cozy atmosphere of a home. She arranges the rooms in the home to include spaces for children's play, for storing play materials in easy reach of the children, for displaying children's work, and for storing children's personal items. In setting up the home, the provider maintains those aspects of the home that help children feel secure and comfortable: sofas, rocking chairs, plants, and personal items are used by family members of all ages. Following are examples of what you should see in family child care homes and why these arrangements of the environment are important.

Environment (cont'd)

What you should see	Why
a childproofed home; electrical outlets covered, loose carpets tacked down, plastic bags and household detergents locked away, stairways protected, cribs out-of-reach of Venetian blind cords, and all toys and the paint on the walls nontoxic	First and foremost, all children must be cared for in a safe, healthy environment. Child-proofing is a basic minimum requirement for providing child care in one's home.
furnishings appropriate to the ages of the children being served—for example, cribs, highchairs, and changing tables for infants; booster chairs for toddlers; and child-size tables and chairs for toddlers, preschoolers, and school-age children	Providers typically care for children of many ages; therefore, a variety of furnishings are needed to match the developmental levels of all of the children in the home. Children need safe, comfortable furnishings that will allow them to master their environment. Child-size tables and chairs, for example, enable a child to easily concentrate on fingerpainting or to learn to feed herself.
areas of the home that are out-of-bounds to the children blocked off by a door, a gate, or a large piece of furniture; breakable objects kept in an out-of-bounds area	When the physical arrangement of the home communicates to children what the boundaries are, the provider does not have to keep reminding children of where they are allowed to be. By making the out-of-bounds areas inaccessible to children, providers help children learn to respect rules. Removing breakable objects is common sense, as well as a positive guidance technique.
spaces in the home available to accommodate individual children's routines and learning needs; for example, uncluttered floors—carpeted and uncarpeted—for infants to practice crawling and walking; quiet places for toddlers, preschoolers, and school-age children to read, do a puzzle, or be alone; and areas set aside for toddlers, preschoolers, and school-age children to engage in noisy activities, such as playing with water, fingerpainting, or engaging in dramatic play; space set aside for sleeping and eating	Children need to have sufficient space, undisturbed by others, to work on projects, develop and practice skills, and participate in activities. They need room to sleep, eat, and explore the environment. To set the stage for growth and development, providers need to arrange their homes to meet the needs, skills, and interests of all of the children in their care. Providers who relegate children to a small bedroom might be protecting their home from wear and tear, but they are also neglecting children's needs.
an outdoor area, or access to an outdoor play area, that can be used for a variety of activities; if the outside play area is not ideal, adaptations that make it safe for children's play; spaces for sand and water play and gardening; swings or climbing apparatus	Children's growth and development are promoted by a variety of outdoor as well as indoor activities. By structuring the outdoor environment so that different types of activities can take place, providers can make the outdoors a learning laboratory.

What you should see	**Why**
an area of the home set up for sharing information with parents; for example, a place where parents can leave a note for the provider on a sign-in sheet, leave a change of clothes for the child where the provider will find it, and pick up their children's take-home art, dirty clothes, and copies of the coming week's schedule and menus	Communication between parents and providers contributes to use of consistent approaches for meeting children's needs. Designating a specific place as a message center enhances communication and recognizes parents as partners in the care and education of their children.
items displayed on walls to stimulate learning; for example, mobiles placed near cribs or changing tables, mirrors hung at children's eye level, and photographs of the children's families and special projects posted for all to see	Children learn from everything in their environment, including items and objects that are hung on the walls. This is particularly important for very young children, who use their senses—including sight—to explore their environment. Carefully selected wall displays will promote learning and stimulate discussion.
children's artwork hung on the walls and the refrigerator at the children's eye level; when the home serves children of varying ages, art displayed at the individual artist's eye level and protected by inexpensive plastic frames or sheets of acetate; if an infant is likely to grab at a "masterpiece," the art either raised out of the would-be "vandal's" reach or protected by a Plexiglas™ frame	When children view their own work on display, they take pride in their accomplishments and feel that their efforts are valued by the provider.
some areas of the home that serve a double function—available to the children during the day, but easily rearranged for use by the provider's family once the children leave for the day	The home is also the provider's family home. Family members will probably be more supportive of the family child care business if their home is arranged so that it can easily revert to family use.
toys and materials stored at the children's level and easily accessible to them; picture and/or word labels indicating where items are stored	When children have easy access to play materials, they can make choices about what they want to do, which helps the children become self-motivated learners. Labeled storage areas encourage children to clean up because they know where items are stored.
personal storage spaces—such as bags hanging on hooks, or plastic crates—provided for children to keep their own personal items, for example, a change of clothes, diapers, hairbrushes, a special blanket, toothbrushes, and towels	Children feel more secure when they are able to bring personal possessions from home and can store these items in places that are easy to reach. Having their own items for brushing their teeth, combing their hair, and so forth, makes the children feel both independent and a part of the family child care "family."

During visits to a family child care home, you can readily observe whether or not the environment is working effectively. If it is, the children will appear busy and happily occupied. On the other hand, if you see children standing around with nothing to do, children who cling to the provider, children who are fighting or screaming, or a provider who seems unable to cope with the children in her care, the environment may be inappropriate. Listed below are warning signs that the environment is not supporting children's growth and development, possible reasons that a provider might have for organizing the environment in these ways, and strategies you might try to help her improve the quality of the environment.

Warning signs	Why this might be happening	How you can help
infants, toddlers, and older children interfering with each other's activities	Younger children don't have a safe space for crawling or toddling; older children don't have areas large enough for moving about; no clear paths allow moving around the play areas in the room; or the provider doesn't use enough rooms in her home for family child care.	Help the provider assess whether the space set aside for family child care is large enough to allow children at different stages of development to move freely. If necessary, help her plan ways to have some double-function areas; for example, she might move the coffee table against a wall during the day so that a baby could safely crawl, then return the coffee table to its spot in front of the couch after the children leave for the day. Also, help the provider create pathways around activity areas so that children can work on projects undisturbed.
children running around the house in circles, squealing excitedly	The rooms in the home probably all connect. Once children discover this, they're off and running.	Work with the provider to restructure the layout so that a circular pathway is no longer available. This might be done by making a room out-of-bounds, moving a piece of furniture in front of a pass-through, or boxing in play areas with furnishings.

Warning signs	Why this might be happening	How you can help
children asking for provider assistance when selecting play materials; children not returning toys and materials to storage areas once they are finished using them	The storage areas are out of the children's reach, or the materials are stored so haphazardly that the children cannot find what they need.	Help the provider design storage areas that are both accessible to the children and organized for easy use. Suggest creating storage areas by using a bookcase, a closet, open shelving, plastic milk cartons, washtubs, or fishnet bags.
toys and other play materials stored in toy boxes; children emptying the box each time they want to use a particular toy	The provider thinks that toy boxes are good storage places because they save space and, once the lid is closed, they hide the "mess."	First, explain to providers that toy boxes are safety hazards—the lids can fall down on children, shutting them inside or hurting their hands. Also, explain that while toy boxes might save space, they do not promote learning. Because toys must be piled into the box, children become frustrated because they cannot readily find what they want. Also, because toys are just thrown in the toy box at cleanup time, children don't learn to sort and classify, as they would if the toys were stored on labeled shelves, and children don't learn to take good care of the toys.

© Marilyn Nolt

Family child care is well suited to the philosophy behind developmental programming. Because of the structure of family child care, every child is always in the forefront. Communication between parents and providers contributes to use of consistent approaches for meeting children's needs.

Warning signs	Why this might be happening	How you can help
pictures, photos, and artwork hanging at adult eye level; children rarely looking at the walls	The provider views artwork as decoration, not an opportunity to promote learning.	Help the provider understand that children feel comfortable in an environment decorated with examples of art that they have created and with photographs and pictures related to current activities and interests. If a provider has difficulty creating an aesthetic arrangement, kneel beside her at the children's height and help her to appropriately post the wall decorations.
children running around the house on bad-weather days	The provider allows children to run freely because they haven't been able to release their pent-up energy outdoors.	Encourage the provider to take the children outdoors as often as possible, even if only for a few minutes on a cold or wet day. Also, work with the provider to think of several ways to incorporate indoor exercise, such as dancing to music or calisthenics, into the daily schedule so that children can release their energy productively without creating chaos. Help the provider find space in her home—perhaps by pushing furniture out of the way—where children can exercise or dance with abandon.
children running or roaming around outdoors without becoming involved in activities	The provider believes that outdoor time is for "letting off steam" and that there is no need to create an outdoor learning environment.	Suggest creating outdoor interest areas—for example, a sand box with sifting and digging tools, an inner tube filled with water and basting tools, a gardening spot, or an old tree trunk for carpentry—where children can play quietly if they choose. Not all outdoor time has to be devoted to gross-motor activity.

Warning signs	Why this might be happening	How you can help
a child with disabilities bumping into furniture, appearing uncomfortable in using the play spaces, or becoming frustrated because he can't reach the materials, toys, and books	The provider hasn't cared for children with disabilities before and has arranged the home in a way that has worked in the past.	Work with the provider to develop a layout that will meet the particular needs of each child in her care. This might require moving furniture, making toys and materials more accessible, widening pass-throughs, or installing pull-away ramps.
one room in the home that has been converted into a minicenter, with interest areas like those in a child development center	Some providers earnestly believe that if their home looks and operates like a center, then they are providing high-quality care.	Help the provider understand how the home environment fosters children's growth and development. Show her how to provide children with experiences like those in a center without creating a minicenter; for example, instead of working at a writing interest area, children can select a basket of paper and writing tools from a shelf and carry it to a low table, where they can explore ways to use the materials.
the provider habitually dressing sloppily, trudging around in slippers or wearing curlers	The provider believes that how she dresses in her own home or in front of very young children does not matter.	Help the provider understand that she is an important part of the environment. How she dresses conveys messages to parents and children about her professional commitment and about the quality of care that she is providing.

Equipment and materials

One of the hallmarks of developmental care is providing materials and equipment that stimulate learning. Family child care providers collect, make, or purchase an inventory of materials and equipment that are appropriate for the ages and developmental levels of the children being served. These inventories are large enough to accommodate the children's needs, skills, and interests, and to encourage all types of development.

Individualizing an inventory

When the children in her care vary in age from newborns to preteens, the provider has on hand a wide range of toys and learning materials. The wider the range of ages served, the more variety of materials provided. A provider who has all infants or all preschoolers in her care will find equipping her home easier than will a provider who cares for children of many ages and stages. Similarly, a provider who cares for a chronically sick child or one with disabilities has materials that address those children's special needs. The task of selecting appropriate materials is thus one that many providers find difficult, especially because acquiring materials for many developmental levels can be expensive. The following suggestions might be helpful.

- Purchased toys and games are not necessarily the best ones. Use household supplies to make variations of popular items, such as puzzles or board games.

- Old wooden furniture, such as tables and chairs, can be sawed down to make them child-size.

- Providers can seek donations for supplies from neighborhood businesses. Many offices are happy to give away used computer paper that can be recycled for art or bookmaking. Wallpaper stores will gladly give away old sample books. It never hurts to ask!

- Providers might form a toy exchange through which materials are shared. This is a cost-effective way to increase the inventories of a group of family child care providers.

- Before purchasing toys or equipment, providers should consider the overall value of the items, asking themselves questions such as,
  - Can the item serve more than one function? (Blocks, for example, can be used to develop coordination, enhance creativity, teach beginning math concepts such as equivalence and spatial relationships, etc.)
  - Can the item be used by more than one of the children in care? (A new crib mobile, for example, can serve only one infant.)
  - Is the material solidly constructed so that it is likely to last?
  - Is the material antibias in nature and in keeping with the values of the children's parents? (Before purchasing something potentially controversial, for example, such as an anatomically correct doll, providers should check with the children's parents.)

© Dena Bawinkel

A suggested list of toys and materials for infants, toddlers, preschoolers, and school-age children, and comments on how a provider might make or obtain them are helpful.

In general, because so many possible choices exist, best practice is to follow the popular wisdom of looking for "the most bang for the buck." An investment in toys and materials should, therefore, only be made when the potential for learning is guaranteed. This implies that purchasing an item of major value, such as a complete set of hardwood unit blocks, might be wiser than buying a number of toys that are of questionable merit.

This section presents a suggested list of items for infants, toddlers, preschoolers, and school-age children, and comments on how a provider might make or obtain them.

Family child care inventory for infants ⎯⎯⎯⎯⎯⎯⎯⎯⎯⎯

Item	Comments
crib mobile	Hang objects such as ribbon, foil, socks, or stuffed animals from a hanger frame to make a homemade mobile. To ensure the infant's safety, hang mobiles so that the infant cannot pull the mobile down by grabbing hold of it.
crib gym	Make crib gyms that infants can reach for, tug at, and hit, from objects such as wooden spoons, spools, and teething rings suspended by string from a wooden dowel.
washable, cuddly toys and stuffed animals	Make stuffed toys from socks (rabbits and monkeys are popular), stockings, or towels filled with old pantyhose or polyester fiberfill.
mirrors	Glue hand-held mirrors from old purses to walls where infants can see their reflections.
rattles	Make rattles by filling plastic containers with poker chips or aluminum baking beads, then taping them shut.
musical toys that children can shake or strike	Make shakers and maracas as described above. Make tambourines by fastening sanded bottle caps to pie tins. Fashion rhythm sticks and jingle sticks out of dowels or old broom handles.
squeak toys, balls of all sizes, and plastic and rubber animals	Buy plastic and rubber animals at flea markets and yard sales.
pull toys	Attach casters and a string to a favorite stuffed animal to make a pull toy.
fill-and-dump toys into which objects are placed and then "dumped" for reuse	Fill plastic containers with clothespins. Suspend the containers by a rope through a ceiling hook for a unique experience.
picture books	Libraries may be a source of cloth books with laminated pages, strong bindings, and illustrations that can be mouthed and touched. Make picture books from magazine pictures, photos of the children's families, or photos of family child care activities, and cover the pages with clear Contact paper.
soft, squeezable blocks	Make soft blocks by covering foam-rubber cubes with terry cloth.

Item	Comments
stacking toys	Inexpensive measuring cups and spoons make ideal toys.
sorting toys	Cut shapes in a shoebox. Provide household objects to drop through the shapes.
simple puzzles of up to three pieces	Make puzzles by gluing magazine pictures or family photos to cardboard, covering the pictures with clear Contact paper, and cutting the pictures into large pieces.
household items, such as pots, spoons, and rubber spatulas, and empty boxes of all sizes	These often make the best toys of all. You may be able to buy them at discount stores on "Dollar Days."

Family child care inventory for toddlers

Any of the materials listed for infants that are still developmentally appropriate for toddlers and are fun to use may be included in the inventory for toddlers, plus the following items.

Item	Comments
hardwood blocks in several sizes	Although expensive to buy, these toys are highly recommended. They are easy to manipulate, and they teach children a number of concepts, from spatial relationships to proportion. You can make them from well-sanded two-by-fours.
magnetic boards	Add kitchen magnets to the boards for variety.
picture books	Borrow books from the library or make them as described above. Make cloth books using nontoxic fabric paint on muslin.
musical instruments for playing and marching with	Use wooden salad bowls as drums. Glue sandpaper to wooden blocks, then rub them together. A thimble can be clanged on a washboard. A comb covered with wax paper can provide harmony.
tapes and CDs of children's music to sing and dance to—classical for resting and rap or rock for exercising	Look in the library or secondhand stores for tapes and CDs of every musical genre.

Item	Comments
take-apart toys with large pieces	Supplement supplies by trading with other providers and looking for sales.
Legos and Bristle Blocks, cause-and-effect toys such as a jack-in-the-box, and toy trucks, buses, and cars	These are frequently available at flea markets and yard sales.
large crayons and paper	Because of their popularity and relatively low cost, crayons are a recommended purchase. Donated newsprint or computer paper makes good drawing paper.
paint, paintbrushes, and paper	Powdered tempera is relatively inexpensive. (Adding a few drops of alcohol or oil of wintergreen will keep it from going sour.) Fingerpaints can be homemade (using 3 c. Vano starch to 1 T. powdered tempera) or bought. Flat bristle brushes work well for beginning painters. Newsprint, construction paper, wrapping paper, and recycled computer paper can all be used in painting.
clay and playdough	Commercial varieties are *not* recommended because they might be harmful if swallowed, and they are difficult to remove from carpets. Homemade recipes are not only cheaper but produce a superior product. A recipe for homemade modeling clay is 1 c. salt, 1½ c. flour, ½ c. warm water, 2 T. oil, and a few drops of food coloring. The traditional playdough recipe is 2 c. flour, 1 c. salt, 2 T. oil, and 1 c. water with food coloring added. A tablespoon of cream of tartar added to the recipe produces a smoother variety of playdough.
beads for stringing	Make these using empty thread spools and give the children shoelaces on which to string the beads.
props for sand play, such as shovels, pails, sifters, strainers, measuring cups and spoons; and props for water play, such as measuring cups, funnels, basting tool, sponge, and floating toys	These items are usually found around the house or at "Dollar Days" sales. Ask parents to save recyclable items.
wagons, tricycles, and other wheeled toys	These often can be found at yard sales.
household items, such as appliance boxes, potting soil and pots, foam-rubber pillow forms, fabric, and felt	A myriad of household items and scraps can be incorporated into science or art projects.

Family child care inventory for preschoolers

Any of the materials listed for infants or toddlers that are still developmentally appropriate for preschoolers and are fun to use may be included in the inventory for preschoolers, plus the following items.

Item	Comments
additional props for sand and water play—for example, squirt bottles, shells, combs, soap flakes, and food coloring—to augment those used by toddlers	These props are usually available in the home.
additional props for dramatic play—for example, brooms, mops, full-length mirrors, plastic dishes, old dressup clothes, hats of all types, gloves, costume jewelry, and accessories related to specific themes, such as grocery stores, offices, or hospitals—to augment those used by toddlers	Many household items can be props. Providers can ask grocery-store managers or hospital administrators to donate accessories, such as paper bags or disposable face masks and gloves, to use as props. Other vendors, such as managers of fast-food outlets, are also good sources for dramatic play materials and costumes.
hardwood unit blocks in proportional sizes	These are an expensive but worthwhile purchase. Providers might buy a basic set, then add to them over time. Children of many ages and stages will play with the blocks, and children rarely tire of block play. Enhance children's play by adding props described below.
additional props for block play—for example, small toy animals, buses, airplanes, cars, doll furniture, traffic signs, pulleys, and trains—to augment those used by toddlers	Most of these props can be purchased at yard sales and flea markets or obtained through exchanges with other providers.
puppets	Make simple versions from socks or rolled newspaper. Use papier mâché for more elaborate puppets.
collectibles—for example, buttons, keys, shells, and leaves	Look for these items around the house or on nature walks.
self-help frames	Use buttons, zippers, Velcro, and laces to fasten two pieces of material together, then stretch and staple the material to a wooden frame
interlocking toys	These can often be picked up at yard sales or exchanged with other providers.
lotto games	Draw or paste lotto boards on cardboard, then cover the cardboard with clear Contact paper.

Item	Comments
sound games	Fill glasses with varying levels of water to produce different sounds when tapped.
shape games	Shape games are usually inexpensive purchases. Cut shapes in appliance boxes through which objects can be placed or for children to crawl through.
writing materials, such as chalk, crayons, markers, and paper	Most of these are inexpensive purchases.
printing materials, such as ink pads and stamps	These inexpensive items are available at stationery or office-supply stores.
woodworking tools, such as a saw, hammer, and nails	Use household tools, not toy versions.
puzzles with more pieces than those used by infants and toddlers	Glue pictures to cardboard, cover them with clear Contact paper, then cut them into pieces.

© Bm Porter/Don Franklin

Children develop self-confidence and independence when they can use materials without adult assistance. Having access to their play materials allows children to make choices about what they want to learn. This builds self-motivation for learning.

Item	Comments
pegs and pegboard	Homemade versions can be made from household supplies.
additional musical instruments—homemade as well as purchased	Earthenware drums and other, more elaborate shakers and rhythm instruments can be made from household supplies and dowels.
books, tapes, and CDs covering topics of interest to children—for example, feelings, social problems, conquering fears, families, growing up	These can be checked out at the library or purchased inexpensively from secondhand stores.
collage materials	Collect household items such as yarn, glitter, feathers, and eggshells for collages.
materials for advanced artwork projects, such as construction paper, glue, a hole punch, a stapler and staples, markers, and rulers	These are usually available in the home and can be returned to the family when the children are finished using them.
animals—for example, fish in an aquarium, birds in a birdhouse, or ants in an ant farm	Inexpensive, easy-to-care-for pets are suggested. Birdhouses can be home-built with assistance, if needed, from a cooperating parent.
plants to grow indoors and outdoors	Buy inexpensive seeds and small plants, ask parents or neighbors for cuttings, or take cuttings from other houseplants. Sprouts and fruits and vegetables that the children can incorporate into cooking activities are highly recommended.
outdoor play materials, such as tires for swings, woodworking tools, and play tools for water, mud, and sand	Such items are often found in the house or garage.
climbing equipment	If no such equipment is available near the provider's home, equipment might be available at a yard sale.
bats, balls, and sports equipment	These can be donated by older children or purchased at yard sales
wheelbarrows and scooters	These items can be purchased at yard sales or found in the home.
additional items that lend themselves to dramatic play, sand and water play, outdoor play, woodworking, science experiments, gardening, or care of a pet	Household items make ready extensions for children's play.

Family child care inventory for school-age children _____

Any of the materials listed for infants, toddlers, or preschoolers that are still developmentally appropriate for school-age children and are fun to use may be included in the inventory for school-age children, plus the following items.

Item	Comments
books, tapes, and CDs appropriate to the children's interests, reading levels, and sophistication	These can be checked out at the library or obtained at used record or CD stores.
writing materials, such as pens, pencils, calligraphy pens and India ink, highlighting pens, a typewriter, and a computer	Household supplies are suggested. Buy additional materials only if they would be valuable for a child. Purchasing a computer for family child care is *not* suggested, but someone might donate an outdated model.
art materials, such as mural paper, fabric paint, wax, fabric, needles and thread, embroidery needles and thread, sew-on sequins, mirrors, and beads	Again, household supplies are suggested. Buy items only if they will be well used by children.
woodworking materials, such as sandpaper and a drill	Again, household supplies are suggested.
sand and water materials, such as glycerin for making bubbles and plaster for making molds	Buy these inexpensive supplies at a hardware store.
a pocket calculator	Most homes have calculators that can be used by older children. Very inexpensive models can be readily purchased if none are available in the home.
a microscope	Because only real equipment is recommended, this expensive item should be used only if one can be donated or borrowed.
a stethoscope	Again, only real ones are suggested. Ask hospitals or doctors to donate old ones.
jump ropes	These are inexpensive purchases. Buy rope at a hardware store, then cut it into desired lengths.
hobby-related paraphernalia—for example, cake decorating tips or computer software	Items found in the house or those received as donations are suggested. Software should be purchased only if it is of interest to more than one child.

Equipment and materials (cont'd) _____

No one family child care home will have this exact inventory of materials, as each provider needs an inventory that matches children's developmental needs and interests with the learning experiences that she believes are important for those children. Your role is to ensure that the provider's inventory works for her and, most importantly, the children in her care. Here are some examples of the equipment and materials you should see when you visit a family child care home and why these items are important.

What you should see	**Why**
materials and equipment appropriate to children's developmental stages—for example, soft, cuddly toys that infants can use their senses to explore; simple puzzles and pull toys for toddlers; dramatic play props and self-help boards that preschoolers can use to practice skills; and books and popular music tapes for school-age children	Children learn through using play materials that are of interest to them and that challenge their minds and bodies without frustrating them. An age-appropriate inventory of equipment and materials allows all of the children in care to play with materials that match their needs, skills, and interests.
materials that provide children with a wide variety of experiences—for example, materials for art, music and movement, cooking, block play, dramatic play, table toys, books and writing experiences, sand and water play, and outdoor play	Children need exposure to a broad base of experiences if they are to develop cognitively, physically, socially, and emotionally.
toys and materials—such as dolls, books, and dramatic play props—that reflect the ethnic and cultural backgrounds of the children in the family child care home and the community	Children learn best when they can identify with the characters in stories they read, the puppets they play with, and the people props they use for dramatic play and block adventures. When they see books and props that look like them, children regard these characters as role models and feel good about themselves. These materials also help children develop a respect for different ethnic groups and cultures.
toys and materials that children can use by themselves—for example, dramatic play props that toddlers and preschoolers can use whenever they like; cuddle toys and rattles within infants' reach; art materials that children can select from a storage shelf	Children develop self-confidence and independence when they can use materials without adult assistance. Having open access to their play materials allows children to make choices about what they want to learn. This, in turn, builds self-motivation for learning.
toys and equipment in good repair, free of jagged edges, rust, dirt, peeling paint, or any other hazards	Children's safety is a primary concern in child care. Children should not have access to any toys or pieces of equipment that are even slightly damaged.

Equipment and materials (cont'd)

What you should see	Why
materials that reflect children's changing skills, needs, and interests	Learning is dynamic in nature. As children grow and develop new interests, they need to use materials that continually challenge them. If they have no new toys or materials to explore, they will soon become bored. Following the first snowfall, a provider might introduce shovels, sleds, and igloo props. She could check out from the library stories about snow adventures and records with songs such as "Frosty the Snowman."
duplicates of popular materials, such as firefighter hats, wheeled toys, and telephones	Learning to share is a developmental process that takes place in early childhood. Infants and toddlers need many opportunities to experience a sense of ownership before they feel secure enough to share; providing duplicates of popular items responds to this need and prevents many disagreements. Preschoolers are better able to wait for a turn using an item; however, at times they, too, are reluctant to share. By the time they reach the school-age years, most children are able to negotiate and find ways to enjoy themselves without squabbling over who gets to use the "best" car.

Learning is dynamic in nature. As children grow and develop new interests, they need to use materials that continually challenge them.

When equipment and materials are inappropriate _____

As you observe in a family child care home, you will easily be able to tell if the provider has selected materials that are age suitable and individually and culturally appropriate. If the home functions well and the children seem creative, busy, and happy, the materials are most likely appropriate; however, if you see frustrated, bored, or unhappy children, the materials and toys may be inappropriate or insufficient. Here are some warning signs that you should look for during your visits and some suggested strategies for helping providers improve the equipment and materials in their homes.

Warning signs	Why this might be happening	How you can help
children seeming bored, ignoring the play materials, running around, pushing each other, or grabbing at the provider for attention	The toys and materials are stored out of children's reach; the children have advanced beyond the developmental levels for which the toys and materials are appropriate; the children have played with the toys so much that they are no longer interested in them; or there aren't enough toys for the children to play with.	Through careful observation and discussions with the provider, try to determine the cause of the problem. If the materials are inappropriate, help the provider see why they aren't working and suggest other toys that she could make that would be better suited to the children's needs. If the materials are inaccessible, work with the provider to create storage sites that are within the children's reach.
children playing with the same materials day after day in routine ways	Children may be repeating actions to gain mastery over the material—which is a part of learning—or they may be bored with the materials and are not really paying attention to them.	Through direct observation you should be able to tell whether the children's repetition occurs thoughtfully or as a result of boredom. If the latter is true, work with the provider to make or obtain materials that are slightly more complex and will therefore challenge the children.
children continually asking the provider how to complete a puzzle, draw a picture, or finish a project they've started	The materials and toys are too difficult for the children, or the children need extra attention from the provider.	Observe the children to see what is taking place. If the materials or projects are too difficult for the children, work with the provider to make or obtain toys that are better suited to the children's skill levels. If the children seem to need attention, discuss this with the provider and suggest ways to help the children feel more secure and confident.

When materials and equipment are inappropriate (cont'd) _____

Warning signs	Why this might be happening	How you can help
children fighting over toys and play materials; everyone wanting to play with the same thing at the same time	The materials and toys lack variety, there aren't enough duplicates of popular items, or the younger children want to do what the older ones are doing.	Observe to determine the cause of the problem. The first two situations can be resolved by working with the provider to offer more variety or to provide duplicates of popular materials. Make sure the provider understands that because most young children are not ready to share, providing duplicates of popular items is best. The latter situation, which is sociodevelopmental in nature, can be resolved through planning. Older children might do activities while the younger children nap, thus avoiding conflict.
few toys and materials available for children to play with; those that are available rarely being changed	The provider has a limited budget for toys and equipment, or she thinks that with fewer materials to play with, the children will make less of a mess.	During a visit to the home, help the provider make toys, such as blocks, puzzles, lotto games, and self-help boards. Bring all of the supplies with you, but encourage the provider to start her own collection of materials for toymaking. Also, help her establish a toy exchange with other providers. A group of providers could assemble rich (but not costly!) inventories of toys and equipment.
walls that are decorated with completed dittos or coloring-book drawings; children using prepackaged learning materials	The provider believes that materials developed by experts are better than the kinds of experiences she could devise.	Discuss with the provider how materials of this type thwart creativity. Help her collect a variety of art materials that children can use in different ways, and show her how to make learning materials, such as lotto games or nesting boxes, that can be used to promote growth and development.

© Stanley Stahr

Children's attention and interest in an activity increases with age; thus, activities for a multi-age group need to be long enough for preschoolers to fully enjoy them but planned so that younger children can take a nap or go on to a new activity on their own.

Warning signs	Why this might be happening	How you can help
children often playing with materials stereotypically—boys building with the blocks and girls cooking and playing house	Children are doing the activities they enjoy, or they have received messages from adults that certain activities are preferable for boys and certain activities are preferable for girls.	Again, observation is called for. If children are engaged in stereotypical behavior because they enjoy it, you don't need to discourage them from playing this way just because we might believe that it doesn't conform to what we'd like them to be doing. The provider can encourage children to try less-stereotyped activities, but the children's own choices should not be ignored. If, however, a provider is directly or indirectly giving children stereotypical messages about sex roles, you should discuss this with her and help her avoid gender bias in the future.
children being admonished for not using scissors or markers correctly—"I told you to hold the marker at the end. Now you have ink all over your hands."	The provider believes that the children are capable of following her directions, or she doesn't realize that toddlers and some preschoolers are not usually developmentally capable of the small-motor control needed for using these implements.	Help the provider developmentally assess the children's fine-motor skills. Suggest strategies that she can use to help children develop these skills— for example, tearing paper, sifting sand, and pouring juice— so that eventually they can master scissors and markers.

Program structure: Schedule and routines _____

Scheduling is one of the most important tasks in planning a family child care program. As with most of family child care, scheduling is tailored to meet the individual needs of the children being served. A home with infants, for example, responds to the babies' individual eating and sleeping schedules. A mixed-age home combines schedules for infants, who need several naps; more active toddlers, who need a little sleep; and preschoolers, who are energy in action. A home providing care for a child with disabilities or a sick child customizes the schedule to accommodate these children's health and physical requirements. In addition, the schedule is flexible to reflect children's growth and changing interests.

The following is a basic framework for a daily schedule that would cover a multi-age grouping. This schedule is a starting point for use with family child care providers—not a finished plan.

*Sample daily schedule for family child care**

Early morning

6:30 - 8:30 A.M.   Children arrive. The provider's own children may be getting ready for school or to begin the day with her. Some children need breakfast. After breakfast, infants are changed and put down to nap.** Children help with cleanup and play with table toys, read books, or listen to story tapes until breakfast and cleanup are finished. School-age children leave for school.

Morning activities

8:30 - 9:30   Toddlers and preschoolers select activities or join in a noisy group activity, such as fingerpainting, water play, cooking, or puppet making. As babies wake up they are brought in to join the group activity. Children help clean up after playtime.

9:30 - 9:45   Snack.

9:45 - 10:45   Get ready to go outside: use the toilet, wash hands, change diapers, and so on. Outdoor play and/or walks; perhaps a science project, such as gardening.

10:45 - 11:15   Free play again—perhaps a special planned activity, such as making and using playdough at the kitchen table.

11:15 - 11:30   Cleanup and storytime; get ready for lunch.

Lunch and rest

11:30 - 12:30 P.M.	Family-style lunch and conversation. After lunch, older children help put food away and clean up. Hands are washed, diapers are changed, and teeth are brushed.
12:30 - 2:30	Everyone (except, perhaps, for a baby who just woke up) has a rest period. Preschoolers who can't sleep rest quietly on their mats or beds for 30 to 40 minutes, looking at a book or playing quietly. They then get up and do a quiet activity. As children wake up, diapers are changed, hands are washed, and hair is combed. Mats are put away.

Afternoon activities

2:30 - 3:00	Children have a snack together, often one they have helped prepare. School-age children arrive and help themselves to a snack. Children discuss choices for afternoon activities. Cleanup follows.
3:00 - 4:00	Active indoor or outdoor play for all children. School-age children are invited to join in. A special project may be planned. Personal cleanup follows, including clothing changes or whatever is necessary to get ready to go home.

Late afternoon/evening

4:00 - 4:45	Free play: Children play with table toys, blocks, or crayons; read books; or build with blocks.
4:45 - 5:00	Group storytime or singing (nondisruptive play for those who don't wish to participate in the group); quiet group activity.
5:00 - 6:00	Children go home at staggered times. Projects are assembled, diapers are changed, and parent information is made ready. Children color, look at books, or play with table toys until their parents arrive. Events of the day and plans for the next day are discussed with children and parents as they leave.

*Adapted with permission from *The Creative Curriculum for Family Child Care* by Diane Trister Dodge and Laura J. Colker (Washington, DC: Teaching Strategies, Inc., 1991), pp. 32-33.

**Infants will nap two and sometimes three times a day on their own schedules, which will change as they grow. Toddlers may take one or two naps each day, often around 10 A.M. and 2 P.M. Like infants, toddlers' sleep demands will change over time and may even increase and decrease at different times. Learning the sleep schedule for each infant is helpful because you can plan active and messy activities that most need your supervision for times when the infants are sleeping.

Program structure: Schedule and routines (cont'd) _____

The following are examples of the program structure you
should see when observing in a family child care home and
explanations of why these items are important.

What you should see	Why
a daily schedule that reflects long-range curriculum goals	Lots of daily activities without direction can lead nowhere. The schedule of daily events ought to reflect a sequenced curriculum. The use of themes, such as "What Makes Us Special" or "Things That Move," is one way to develop a curriculum framework.
scheduled activities that are appropriate for the developmental levels of the children served; group activities that are planned so that younger children can leave the activity when they become bored and older children can continue until they are finished	Children's attention and interest in an activity increases with age; thus, activities for a multi-age group need to be long enough for preschoolers to fully enjoy them but planned so that younger children can take a nap or go on to a new activity on their own. Children should be encouraged to participate in group activities only to the extent that they are interested and capable of doing so. Forcing young children to keep still while older children finish up does not work.
infants allowed to keep individual schedules; activities for older children planned with this in mind	Infants need to sleep, be changed, and be fed according to their bodies' time clocks, not an imposed schedule. Providers who care for infants must respond to infants' individual schedules while still accommodating the needs of older children.
the provider spending time each day talking and working with individual children	One of the unique benefits of family child care is that the adult-to-child ratio is low. This permits providers to know each child as an individual and to nurture each child's growth in a loving way. Providers need schedules that are not so action packed that they do not have time to relate to each child throughout the day. When an infant wakes up while older children are building with blocks, for example, the provider can cuddle the infant while talking to the older children about their tower.

What you should see	**Why**
a schedule that includes activities led by the provider and activities selected by the children	Although children need to make their own choices about what they want to play with, providers can also plan and lead activities that reinforce and extend children's self-selected play activities.
a schedule that shows a balance between quiet and active times	Children need times to express themselves actively and times to participate in quiet, soothing activities. Most children's body schedules make them predisposed to quiet activities first thing in the morning, right after lunch, and before they leave for the day. After napping, children need opportunities to let out their restored energy.
children participating in and learning from routines and transitions, such as diapering, preparing lunch, cleaning up, zipping coats, and carrying materials outdoors	Participating in routines and transitions helps children develop self-help skills, which in turn helps them feel competent and independent. In addition, routines and transitions are excellent opportunities for learning and for one-on-one time with the provider.
a schedule that is flexible enough to accommodate the unforeseen "teachable moment"—for example, a hailstorm, a rainbow, or a visitor	Gaps in scheduling leave too much to chance, but an inflexible schedule does not allow the provider to take advantage of "teachable moments." By responding to the children's excitement when snow starts falling, for example, a provider can easily motivate children to learn.
the schedule posted where parents and children can see it; a picture version (photos or drawings) also posted so that children can understand the schedule and anticipate what will come next	Parents are comforted by knowing that their children are following a well-planned schedule. When children are familiar with the schedule, they can predict the day's events. This helps them feel secure and in control of the day. Security, in turn, leads to independence and self-control.
the provider and parents sharing information about children during arrival and departure times	Good communication between parents and providers is essential so that all caregivers have accurate information about the child and can provide individualized care. Providers can reinforce parents' role as primary educators of their children by building time into their schedules for talking with the children's parents at the beginning and end of the day.

When the program structure is not working _____

A daily schedule that is not working well will most likely be obvious. A structure that breaks down is an invitation to frustration and chaos. Here are the signs that will tell you that the program structure is not working as it should and some suggested strategies for helping providers develop schedules that will be more effective.

Warning signs	Why this might be happening	How you can help
children wandering around aimlessly, without settling down with a toy or joining in an activity	The provider doesn't follow a daily schedule, or the schedule uses blocks of time that are too long for the children's attention spans.	If the provider does not have a schedule, give her a copy of the one included in this chapter as an example, and help her devise one that is appropriate for the children in her care. If the provider uses a schedule with long blocks of time unaccounted for, help her develop one that has shorter time slots for activities. Self-selected activity times, for example, can become overwhelming to children if they go on for longer than an hour without some sort of direction.
the provider making all of the children participate in group projects, such as painting a mural or making candles; children who don't want to join in, crying or disturbing others; infants crawling into the middle of the project, ruining everyone's time	The provider thinks that all of the children, no matter what their ages, benefit from the group experience, or she finds supervising children easier when they're all in one area of the home doing the same thing.	Help the provider plan a group activity that has something for everyone, based on individual interests and skill levels. Make sure that other choices exist for children who don't want to participate (for example, painting individually rather than making a mural). Encourage the provider to schedule for the babies' naptime group projects that might be disturbed by infants.

Warning signs	Why this might be happening	How you can help
the provider continually cleaning up after the children and doing things for them that they could do for themselves	The provider doesn't want to interrupt the children's activities, or she thinks that she wouldn't be providing high-quality care if she had children do things for themselves.	Ask the provider to think about a time when she learned to do something new and how proud she felt when she mastered the task (for example, programming the VCR). Explain that children also benefit from learning self-help skills. Participating in routines, such as cleaning up is a part of learning that teaches children responsibility, independence, and cognitive skills. Encourage the provider to let everyone participate in routines, according to their abilities. Even an infant can return a toy to the shelf when she or he is finished playing.
lunchtime going on for hours, often taking up half of the day	The provider believes in letting children eat according to their own time clocks.	Help the provider understand that while infants should be fed on demand, only one hour of the day is needed for family-style dining. The lunch hour is not just a time for eating but for being together, sharing confidences, and enjoying each other's company. Even an infant who has just eaten can have a bottle of juice or water while the older children eat. To keep it special, though, lunch should be limited to an hour from serving to cleanup.
children following a schedule that parallels almost exactly what goes on in a child development center	The provider believes that following a center's schedule will ensure that her program provides the "right" kinds of activities and experiences.	Ask the provider to review her schedule and think about what children are learning at different times of the day and during different activities and routines. Help her understand that a high-quality family child care home takes its scheduling cues from the children served and reflects the home environment.

Warning signs	Why this might be happening	How you can help
children who are too excited or wound up from play to take a nap	The provider believes in giving children lots of stimulation and sees this as a sign that her program is working.	Help the provider to view naptime as an integral and valuable part of the day's activities. Infants nap according to individual time clocks. Toddlers and preschoolers usually nap after lunch, which provides a natural transition from this activity. Work with the provider to develop rituals— to be repeated each day—that help children settle down for their naps. These might include getting out blankets and stuffed animals, playing soft music, rubbing backs, and listening to a short poem.
children who are so wound up at the end of the day that they sometimes break into tears when they see their parents	Children are overtired because their naps were too short; they aren't prepared to leave because they just came in from outdoors, where they've been running around; or they are involved in a favorite activity.	Help providers to better balance their daily schedule so that children don't end the day exhausted or at a high pitch. Favorite activities should be scheduled earlier in the day, when children have ample opportunity to play and complete their work. The end of the day is another time when rituals can be helpful. Help providers develop a plan for ending each day in the same calm and relaxing way.
the provider keeping to the written schedule within two to three minutes of each event	The provider believes that by following her schedule to the minute, she is offering a well-planned, high-quality program.	Help the provider understand that while planning is crucial, a rigid schedule does not allow children to feel as though they have accomplished their goals. A child might need extra time to work on a block construction or to finish baking muffins.

Activities and experiences _____

In a high-quality family child care home, the children's day includes a variety of activities and experiences. Children are involved in routines and transitions, engage in free play, explore the environment, and participate in provider-led activities. When observing in a family child care home, you will see children actively involved in many kinds of experiences. Listed below are examples of the kinds of activities and experiences that typify an appropriate family child care program and the reasons why these activities and experiences are important.

What you should see

children participating in activities that are developmentally appropriate for their ages and stages—for example, infants picking up finger foods, toddlers putting napkins on the table, preschoolers and school-age children peeling and cutting carrots

Why

Children learn best when they can participate in ways that reflect their capabilities. Family child care must provide opportunities for children to be involved at a challenging but not overwhelming level.

© Karen Lee Ensley

Children need to make sense of their world and the people in it. This begins in infancy, as infants develop relationships with parents and caregivers, and continues as children learn to play alone and with others. These activities help children learn important social skills.

Activities and experiences (cont'd)

What you should see	Why
children participating in activities that encourage socioemotional growth—for example, an infant watching and listening to the provider as she changes a diaper, toddlers pretending to call their parents on the telephone, preschoolers working together on a block structure, and school-age children planning a puppet show	Children need to make sense of their world and the people in it. This begins in infancy, as infants develop relationships with parents and caregivers, and continues as children learn to play alone and with others. These activities help children learn important social skills.
children participating in activities that promote cognitive development—for example, infants playing peek-a-boo with older children, toddlers matching shapes and colors, preschoolers measuring ingredients for bread, and school-age children working together to plan next week's snack menus	Children develop cognitive skills as they explore materials, discover concepts, make decisions, solve problems, and interact with others. Activities such as these help children develop and apply thinking skills.
children participating in activities that encourage the development of gross-motor skills—for example, infants crawling, stretching, and standing; toddlers and preschoolers jumping, hopping, climbing, and running; and school-age children playing double-Dutch jump rope	Children thrive physically when they can use their bodies. They develop their gross-motor skills when they have many opportunities to move around in their environment.
children participating in activities that encourage fine-motor skills—for example, infants picking up pieces of food from their high-chair trays, toddlers stringing large beads, preschoolers cutting paper for collages, and school-age children weaving potholders	Children need to participate in increasingly difficult activities that improve their fine-motor skills and eye-hand coordination. Activities such as these allow children to develop and refine their small-motor skills.
providers working one-on-one with children	The low adult-child ratio in family child care allows providers to give individual attention to each child. This lets children know that they are valued and appreciated and contributes to the development of self-esteem.
providers asking children open-ended questions about what they are doing and encouraging children to try new things	When providers reinforce and extend children's learning by asking open-ended questions, they are encouraging children to predict, compare, and apply old knowledge to new situations.

What you should see	**Why**
children selecting what they want to play with and returning materials when they are finished using them	Children develop a sense of independence and responsibility when allowed to make choices about what they want to do and when they can clean up when finished using materials.
children playing outdoors in the provider's yard or at a nearby playground	The outdoor environment is ideal for active play. It also provides a change of pace for activities that usually take place indoors, such as eating lunch or snack, painting at easels, using a prop box, and playing board games.
older children helping younger children	Family child care provides numerous opportunities for older children to serve as models for younger ones. In most instances, both will benefit. Younger children tend to prefer learning from a slightly older child, and older children like showing a younger child how to do something they've already mastered. This is especially true when school-age children are in the home because the younger children tend to look up to these older children.
children participating in activities that take advantage of the home environment, both indoors and outdoors—for example, sorting socks out of the dryer, timing a hard-boiled egg, greeting the mail carrier, watering a plant, or feeding a pet	As a rule, many family child care activities can be an outgrowth of what occurs naturally in the home. Activities such as these encourage the development of specific skills and allow children of different ages to participate at a level appropriate to their capabilities.
the provider and the children taking a walk around the neighborhood	Children of all ages enjoy the change of scenery provided by a neighborhood walk, with many interesting things to see and listen to—daffodils popping up in spring, construction vehicles breaking ground for a new house, or an ambulance on its way to an emergency.

When the activities are inappropriate

If the activities being offered in a family child care home do not help children grow and develop, you need to help the provider plan activities that are more developmentally appropriate. The following are warning signs that the activities and learning experiences are not well suited to the children and some suggested strategies for helping providers improve their programs.

Warning signs	Why this might be happening	How you can help
the provider leading activities that focus almost solely on intellectual growth—for example, singing alphabet songs, playing lotto games, using blocks to demonstrate geometry concepts, and conducting science experiments	The provider believes that by stressing cognitive development she is helping prepare children for school.	Share with the provider some of the research on school readiness that shows that children need to participate in activities that will promote their socioemotional and physical growth, as well as their cognitive growth, to be well prepared for later academic learning. In addition, explain how children's pretend play with props allows them to discover important concepts that they will use when they are old enough for academic learning.
children playing with the same materials expected to master the same learning goals at the same pace	The provider doesn't understand that children progress at their own paces and, therefore, take different amounts of time to learn new skills.	Help the provider plan individualized activities for each child; for example, she might focus on helping one child learn spatial relationships by matching blocks to picture labels. The activity for another child might focus on pairing unit blocks to show equivalence.
the provider completing children's work—puzzles, block towers, art projects, or math homework—for them	The provider doesn't want children to become frustrated and quit trying. She thinks that children want her to help.	Ask the provider to consider how she feels (frustrated? incompetent? annoyed?) when someone tries to help her complete a task without first asking her if she needs their help. Explain that children develop self-confidence by doing things for themselves. Also, point out that it's best to offer assistance only when asked. Even then, the provider needs to be on the alert to determine if the project or puzzle is too advanced for the child.

Warning signs	Why this might be happening	How you can help
the provider offering mostly group activities	The provider believes that children learn best from group experiences, or she finds supervision less of a hassle when all of the children are together in one place.	While you don't want to discourage providers from doing group activities, point out that children also need the experience of playing in groups of two, playing alone, and playing together with the provider. An effective program needs a balance of approaches.
the provider keeping infants confined to walkers and jumpers	The provider uses the walker or jumper to maintain order in the home and cut down on messes created by babies, or she thinks that spending time confined in such equipment is good for infants.	Explain to the provider that young children learn by using their senses to explore their environment. Equipment that keeps children confined prevents them from moving about and limits their development.

© Graham Bell

While you don't want to discourage providers from doing group activities, point out that children also need the experience of playing in groups of two, playing alone, and playing together with the provider. An effective program needs a balance of approaches.

Warning signs	Why this might be happening	How you can help
group activities centered on making a product to take home	The provider wants children to have a finished product to show their parents each day as evidence that she is doing a good job and that the children are enjoying family child care.	First, help the provider understand that young children learn through the process of doing an activity and often are not interested in the products of their efforts. Next, help her role-play explaining to parents that what their children are learning is more important than what they produce. Show her how to conduct experiments with magnets, invent musical notes, or tap the sun's energy—all of which are activities that do not have "products."
children choosing the same activities day after day	Children like these activities so much that they keep at them day after day; they are practicing skills that they are not yet comfortable with; or they don't know what else to do.	Conduct joint observations with the provider, then review each set of recordings together to determine the root of this behavior. If children enjoy the activities or are still experimenting, encourage the provider to reinforce children's play and then gently extend it. If children are repeating the same activities because they don't know what else to do, show the provider how to steer the children to new, stimulating activities.
children glued to the television set, watching cartoons, viewing videotaped movies, or playing electronic games	The provider uses television as a babysitter while she cooks dinner or does other household chores.	Help the provider understand that while certain television programs are indeed educational, the experience of television viewing is far too passive for young children, who need to be actively engaged in play. Help her find ways to involve children in everyday activities, such as cooking or watering plants. Children will see these as interesting experiences, not as chores.

© Dena Bawinkel

Warm, nurturing care is beneficial for children of all ages. It makes them feel important and valued by their provider. Positive encouragement helps children learn which behaviors are acceptable and which ones are not, and helps them learn to develop inner control.

Supportive interactions

Many of the topics discussed earlier in this chapter are challenging for providers who must deal with the complexities and special requirements of providing developmental care for children in a multi-age setting. Supportive interactions, however, is one area that is probably easier for a provider to address because most home environments naturally foster the development of children's self-esteem. A skilled family child care provider encourages children's growth and development through her use of positive guidance techniques, through her attention to children's individual needs, and through interactions that support and extend children's learning.

Here are some examples of the kinds of supportive actions that you should see on your visits to family child care homes and the reasons why these interactions are important.

What you should see	Why
the provider giving individual attention to each child—for example, smiling back at an infant, hugging a crying toddler, rocking with a child in the rocking chair, or listening to a school-age child tell about what happened at school	Warm, nurturing care is beneficial for children of all ages. It makes them feel important and valued by their provider.
the provider giving children information about upcoming transitions ("It will be pickup time in five minutes") rather than making threats of punishment ("Hurry up; put these toys away right now or you won't get any lunch") to help children prepare for these changes	Some children need time to adjust to transitions from one activity to the next. The five-minute warning allows them to finish their play and adjust to the upcoming change. It also allows them to learn self-control because they are responsible for bringing their own play to a close rather than having to respond to the provider's command.
the provider involving children in defining appropriate limits, communicating these to children, and enforcing them consistently	When children are involved in setting rules and limits, they are more likely to understand the reasons for the rules and will be more willing to follow them. This positive guidance technique helps children learn to control their own behavior rather than being dependent on the provider. Clarity and consistency make rules seem fair to children.
the provider giving children positive encouragement for appropriate behavior, not using threats or punishment	Positive encouragement helps children learn which behaviors are acceptable and which ones are not, and helps them learn to develop inner control. Children faced with threats and punishment tend to behave because they fear the consequences of misbehavior, not because they have self-discipline.

What you should see	Why
the provider intervening when one child hits another, bites another, or otherwise loses control	When children's behavior is out of control, the provider needs to step in, comfort the victim, and gently but firmly restrain and redirect the out-of-control child. She needs to let all of the children know what is and what is not appropriate social behavior.
the provider encouraging children to be independent—for example, during self-selected activities children choose their own materials; clean up after themselves; and participate in preparing, serving, and cleaning up meals and snacks; and the provider helps children master self-help boards and learn to dress themselves	Children who are secure and confident learn to be independent and in control of their own lives. Helping children to become self-sufficient is an important part of a provider's role.
the provider comforting children when they are afraid, frustrated, startled, or unhappy; and helping them feel secure	Children of all ages need the security of a trusted adult to see them through a period of anxiety. Out of this sense of security will eventually emerge autonomy.
the provider commenting with considered thought on some aspect of children's projects or activities—for example, "I see you holding the bottle by yourself"; "The bright colors in your picture are very cheerful"; "Choosing a squirrel as the character in your story was a very original idea"; or "Your block tower looked as though it was tall enough to reach the ceiling"	Children feel good about themselves when adults notice and comment on their activities and accomplishments. Positive reinforcement that is offered genuinely helps children feel ready to take on new challenges and learn new skills.
the provider talking to infants and nonverbal toddlers throughout the day, just as she talks to older children	Children learn to communicate when adults communicate with them. Communication— even with preverbal children—builds a foundation for language and strengthens the children's bond with the provider.
the provider treating each child as an individual and encouraging that child's strengths, interests, and talents	Each child is a unique human being. In recognizing this and encouraging each child's special characteristics, providers help children expand their capabilities and develop self-esteem.
the provider keeping parents informed on all aspects of the program and their child's progress and asking parents to share with her information about the children's home activities	Parents have valuable information about their children to share with the provider. If parents are actively involved, they are likely to reinforce the priorities of the family child care program for children at home and are likely to have a continued interest in their children's progress at family child care. Children, likewise, feel good about being in family child care when they see their parent and their provider supporting one another.

FAMILY CHILD CARE

When interactions are inappropriate

You are likely to observe many positive social interactions in family child care homes; however, not every provider will always be positive nor will every home have an environment that fosters children's self-esteem and social skills. Here are some examples of warning signs that the interactions in a family child care home are not appropriate and suggestions for helping the provider be more supportive.

Warning signs	Why this might be happening	How you can help
the provider banning a child from a popular activity, such as blowing bubbles or storytime, because the child didn't respond to her request to clean up	The provider believes that children will learn to behave appropriately if they are deprived of activities they enjoy and thus have time to reflect on their misbehavior.	Work with the provider to help her understand the theory behind positive guidance. Punishment such as this is too harsh for a young child, is damaging to a child's socioemotional well-being, and does not help the child learn how to behave in accepted ways.
the provider forcing a child to eat all of his vegetables at lunch or depriving him of dessert because he pushed another child	The provider believes that food rewards and punishment can effectively control children's behavior.	Work with the provider to develop an approach to discipline that does not focus on external controls. Also, help the provider understand that by using food in this way she is helping children develop poor nutrition habits.
the provider reacting to a child's misbehavior without attempting to find out the cause of the child's actions	The provider doesn't understand that there are causes for children's misbehavior that need to be pinpointed so that she can respond in a way that will help the child stop the objectionable behavior.	Discuss how responding to misbehavior without searching for the cause is like putting a Bandaid® on a gushing wound. Help the provider learn to observe the child, seek information from the child's parents, assess the environment, and so forth. Was the child testing limits? Does the child need extra attention because of something happening at home? Is the environment inappropriate? Have the rules been communicated to the child?

Warning signs	Why this might be happening	How you can help
the provider giving children inconsistent discipline or attention and interacting with some children more than with others	The provider genuinely likes some of the children in her care more than others.	Help the provider understand that she has a commitment to provide developmentally appropriate care to all of the children in her program. Discuss with the provider appropriate ways of dealing with neutral or negative feelings about individual children. Also, point out how preferential, inconsistent behavior has a negative effect on all of the children.
the provider lavishing children with compliments on how they look or dress—"You look so cute today with your pretty red ribbons matching your red sweater."	The provider believes that complimenting children on their looks and clothes builds the children's self-confidence.	Discuss with the provider that although some comments about children's appearance are appropriate, daily compliments are not. Children need to feel valued for who they are—not what they look like or the clothes they are wearing.
the provider talking to infants and toddlers in baby talk	The provider thinks that babies and toddlers will not understand "real" words.	Model appropriate language for the provider to use when talking to children of all ages.
the provider making disparaging remarks about the children's parents to another adult in front of the children	The provider honestly feels this way and thinks that the children will not hear or pay attention to her negative remarks.	Help the provider understand that parents are the most important people in young children's lives. For a provider to say—even indirectly—negative things about these beloved ones is confusing and overwhelming to a young child. Discuss this with the provider and enlist her cooperation in this area.

Resources for working in family child care homes ———

The Children's Foundation. (1991). *Helping children love themselves and others: A professional handbook for family day care*. Washington, DC: Author.

Written with providers in mind, this publication focuses on diversity and multicultural issues. The book includes activities for children, an extensive bibliography, and a unique calendar of multicultural holidays.

Dodge, D.T., & Colker, L.J. (1991). *The creative curriculum for family child care*. Washington, DC: Teaching Strategies.

An environmentally based curriculum that provides practical strategies for setting up the home and planning a program that meets children's developmental needs. Includes nine types of activities that providers can plan for children to promote their growth and learning. Four age-specific activity posters and a videotape and user's guide, *Caring and Learning,* are also available.

Dombro, A.L., & Bryan, P. (1991). *Sharing the caring*. New York: Simon & Schuster.

Parents and providers are encouraged to be aware of their feelings about sharing the care of young children. The authors offer practical suggestions of ways to build partnerships that will help children feel safe and secure in child care.

Dombro, A.L., Colker, L.J., & Dodge, D.T. (1997). *The creative curriculum for infants and toddlers*. Washington, DC: Teaching Strategies.

Provides a comprehensive yet easy-to-use framework for planning and implementing a developmentally appropriate program for infants and toddlers. Can be used in center-based and family child care settings. Accompanied by a journal for caregivers/teachers implementing the curriculum.

Dombro, A.L., & Wallach, L. (1988). *The ordinary is extraordinary: How children under three learn*. New York: Simon & Schuster.

A look at the world through the eyes of infants and toddlers. Readers see how children learn physical, cognitive, emotional, and social skills by participating in daily routines with their parents and providers.

Gonzalez-Mena, J. (1991). *Tips and tidbits: A book for family day care providers*. Washington, DC: NAEYC.

This is a collection of "bits and pieces" of practical strategies and suggestions that can help family child care providers in their daily work with children. Each section includes a bibliography of additional readings.

Gonzalez-Mena, J., & Widmeyer, D.E. (1997). *Infants, toddlers, and caregivers*. Palo Alto, CA: Mayfield.

An insightful look at life in a child care setting. In addition to learning about who children are at different ages, providers will come to appreciate that there is nothing more important than their relationships with the children they care for.

Koralek, D.G., Colker, L.J., & Dodge, D.T. (1993). *Caring for children in family child care*. Washington, DC: Teaching Strategies.

This comprehensive, self-instructional training program is designed specifically to address the training needs of family child care providers. The two-volume set includes 13 models based on the CDA functional areas, along with a trainer's guide.

Lubchenko, A. (1981). *Spoonful of lovin': A manual for day care providers*. Bloomington, IN: Agency for Instructional Television.

This extensive manual can be used on its own or as an accompaniment to the television series of the same name. It gives providers practical how-to suggestions on caring for children from birth through school age. Appendices provide instructions for making toys, dealing with special needs, and maintaining records.

Miller, K. (1984). *Things to do with toddlers and twos,* and (1990) *More things to do with toddlers and twos*. Marshfield, MA: Telshare.

In these two books Karen Miller shares her deep understanding of and affinity for toddlers, which is based on many years of experience as a teacher and trainer. Each book contains more than 500 tips and activities, all of which can be implemented using basic materials found in almost any home.

Miller, K. (1985). *Ages and stages*. Marshfield, MA: Telshare.

Describes clearly the stages that children pass through as they develop physically, emotionally, and intellectually and offers suggestions for how providers can respond to meet children's needs and encourage their growth and development.

Osborn, H. (1994). *Room for loving, room for learning: Finding the space you need in your family child care home*. St. Paul, MN: Redleaf.

This book is filled with diagrams and practical advice on how to set up for family child care, no matter what type of home, and using the space available.

Weitzman, E. (1992). *Learning language and loving it*. Toronto: Hanen Centre.

Based on an on-site training program for early childhood staff, this book covers language learning from birth through the preschool years. Clear and vivid examples, illustrations, and graphics make the book practical and readable.

Audiovisual resources

Colker, L.J. (1995). *Observing young children: Learning to look, looking to learn.* Washington, DC: Teaching Strategies.

This 30-minute videotape and accompanying user's guide train staff and providers on how to objectively and accurately observe children. Viewers gain skills in focusing their observations in order to learn more about children, to measure children's progress, and to evaluate the effectiveness of their program.

Duffy, C. (Producer), & Dodge, D.T., & Colker, L.J. (Directors). (1990). *Caring and learning.* Washington, DC: Teaching Strategies.

A 23-minute video that shows how four providers from different backgrounds offer high-quality family child care. It illustrates how providers use the nine activity areas described in *The Creative Curriculum for Family Child Care* to help children grow and learn.

Further resources from NAEYC*

Baker, A.C. (1992). A puzzle, a picnic, and a vision: Family day care at its best. *Young Children, 47*(5), 36-38.

DeBord, K. (1993). A little respect and eight more hours in the day: Family child care providers have special needs. *Young Children, 48*(4), 21-26.

Manfredi/Petitt, L.A. (1991). Ten steps to organizing the flow of your family day care day. *Young Children, 46*(3), 14-16.

Modigliani, K., Reiff, M., & Jones, S. (1987). Opening your door to children: How to start a family day care program. Washington, DC: NAEYC.

A warm, readable book discussing everything you could possibly want to know about starting up your *own* program.

Trawick-Smith, J., & Lambert, L. (1995). The unique challenges of the family child care provider: Implications for professional development. *Young Children, 50*(3), 25-32.

*To obtain a book published by NAEYC, call 800-424-2460 and ask for Resource Sales. For *Young Children* articles from the past five years, call the Institute for Scientific Information, 215-386-0100, ext. 5399, or fax 215-222-0840; from earlier issues, contact NAEYC's Public Affairs Department.

Early years are learning years

Become a member of NAEYC, and help make them count!

Just as you help young children learn and grow, the National Association for the Education of Young Children—your professional organization—supports you in the work you love. NAEYC is the world's largest early childhood education organization, with a national network of local, state, and regional Affiliates. We are more than 100,000 members working together to bring high-quality early learning opportunities to all children from birth through age eight.

Since 1926, NAEYC has provided educational services and resources for people working with children, including:

• *Young Children,* the award-winning journal (six issues a year) for early childhood educators

• **Books, posters, brochures, and videos** to support your work with young children and families

• **The NAEYC Annual Conference,** which brings tens of thousands of people together from across the country and around the world to share their expertise and ideas on the education of young children

• **Insurance plans** for members and programs

• **A voluntary accreditation system** to help programs reach national standards for high-quality early childhood education

• **Young Children International** to promote global communication and information exchanges

• **www.naeyc.org**—a dynamic Website with up-to-date information on all of our services

To join NAEYC

To find a complete list of membership benefits and options or to join NAEYC online, visit **www.naeyc.org/membership.** Or you can mail this form to us.

(Membership must be for an individual, not a center or school.)

Name _____

Address_____

City_____ State_____ ZIP_____

E-mail _____

Phone (H)_____(W)_____

❏ New member

❏ Renewal ID # _____

Affiliate name/number _____

To determine your dues, you must visit **www.naeyc.org/membership** or call 800-424-2460, ext. 2002.

Indicate your payment option

❏ VISA   ❏ MasterCard

Card # _____

Exp. date _____

Cardholder's name _____

Signature _____

Note: By joining NAEYC you also become a member of your state and local Affiliates.

Send this form and your payment to

NAEYC
PO Box 97156
Washington, DC 20090-7156